FULFILLED

Advance Praise for

FULFILLED

"Will Schirmer's new book *Fulfilled: Finding Joy and Prosperity in Life* is a terrific read that discusses the skills, resources, and techniques anyone can employ to find greater happiness in their lives. From discussing the importance of Character to Emotional Intelligence and Resilience, *Fulfilled* is a great reference tool as you find your way in life."

John G. Miller, Author of *QBQ! The Question Behind the Question* and *Outstanding! 47 Ways to Make Your Organization Exceptional*

"William Schirmer's book, *Fulfilled: Finding Joy and Prosperity in Life,* is a very insightful and practical guide for increasing your fulfillment in life and career in a blanched, meaningful and sustainable manner regardless of life's ups and downs you come across. Drawing on his vast experience and current thought leaders, he leads you through new mindsets and self-awareness activities to expand your consciousness for all aspects of personal growth and transformation."

Mark Samuel, Author of *The Power of Personal Accountability* and *Making Yourself Indispensable*

FULFILLED
Finding Joy &
Prosperity in Life

WILL SCHIRMER

NEW YORK

LONDON • NASHVILLE • MELBOURNE • VANCOUVER

FULFILLED
Finding Joy & Prosperity in Life

© 2022 WILL SCHIRMER

Published in New York, New York, by Morgan James Publishing. Morgan James is a trademark of Morgan James, LLC. www.MorganJamesPublishing.com

Proudly distributed by Ingram Publisher Services.

Morgan James BOGO™

A **FREE** ebook edition is available for you or a friend with the purchase of this print book.

CLEARLY SIGN YOUR NAME ABOVE

Instructions to claim your free ebook edition:
1. Visit MorganJamesBOGO.com
2. Sign your name CLEARLY in the space above
3. Complete the form and submit a photo of this entire page
4. You or your friend can download the ebook to your preferred device

ISBN 978-1-63195-657-7 paperback
ISBN 978-1-63195-658-4 ebook
Library of Congress Control Number:
2021910405

Cover Design by:
Rachel Lopez
www.r2cdesign.com

Morgan James PUBLISHING Builds with... **Habitat for Humanity** Peninsula and Greater Williamsburg

Morgan James is a proud partner of Habitat for Humanity Peninsula and Greater Williamsburg. Partners in building since 2006.

Get involved today! Visit MorganJamesPublishing.com/giving-back

TABLE OF CONTENTS

ACKNOWLEDGMENTS

Many individuals directly or indirectly inspired the content of this book. The content grew from leadership development programs my teams and I implemented in organizations over the years. The foundational level was a course on self-leadership, preparing aspiring managers for the journey by teaching them first how to successfully lead themselves. Along the way I came to realize that the content really applied as a guide for finding fulfillment, happiness, and prosperity in our lives—not just during the workday. And so, the concept for the book was born. Daniel Hinsley, Keryn Rowland, Brad Noel, Tim Cruciani, Bob Schoofs, Garland Koch, Ken Brossman, Mark Rieland, Magali Delafosse, Paul Worachek, Mark Murtha, and Butch Fuller were bosses and executive colleagues who left indelible impressions on me over the years with their integrity, wisdom, support, and kindness. I worked with a couple of them all too briefly, but real class never takes long to make its mark.

I've been fortunate enough to work with a number of excellent colleagues in Human Resources, Learning and Development, and Talent Management over the years. These individuals were extremely supportive and hardworking teammates who also contributed to my personal and professional growth. They include: Denise Johnson, Rick Klein, Crystal Everson, Erin Mueller, Casey Schmidt, Ann Sandstrom, Kaitlyn Dorn, Brent Wood, Eileen Girling, Joe Bembnister, Bob Benzinger, Areti Xioura, Joy Abogado, Rob Van Craenenbroeck, Lynn Sumpter, Ben Wickerham, and Petr Gistinger. There are a number of others, including my HR colleagues at Heartland Financial, who I was very fortunate to call teammates.

In addition, I'd like to thank Morgan James Publishing and also my book editor, Aubrey Kosa, who helped me transform my work into something I'm proud to represent as mine and that I hope you find valuable as a reference point on your life's journey.

My parents, who have both passed on, left the biggest impression on me through the life lessons they taught about love and caring, selflessness, responsibility, and integrity. I'm very appreciative of my sister, Cathy, and brother-in-law and Vern Hagstrom, whose support during the time of this book's writing has been particularly important in my life. I am also, of course, very grateful for the love and support of both family and friends over the years. A big thank you also to my long-time friends Stephen Coskran and Peter Foley. Although we don't talk as much as we should, you helped keep me grounded and sane during what has been a busy and eventful couple of years!

PREFACE

We often go chasing happiness without an understanding of what that really means to us. Life is certainly a journey, and part of that experience is exploring what makes us happy—and what has the opposite effect. Sometimes a lack of reflection on our experiences leads us to stumble along, taking long, winding roads toward fulfillment and prosperity when a shorter route is available. Time is a precious commodity. We cannot manufacture more of it, so finding the shortest distance from today to personal fulfillment tomorrow seems wise. That is what this book is about: finding a quicker route to happiness and prosperity that is less littered with obstacles and turns—and navigating through such challenges and detours when they are encountered.

Now, I can't tell you how to be happy and fulfilled, nor can I tell you how to live a rich life (in whatever way you define prosperity). This book isn't a cure-all for that most human of quests: finding our own city of gold. Life isn't a game of chess; I'm afraid it's much more complicated than that. In some ways it has far fewer rules, and in some senses many more. There is no neat process map or ten-step guide to happiness. Together, however, we can explore the aspects of your personality and competencies that may influence your happiness and fulfillment.

I don't have all the answers for my own life—or yours. Through my trials, errors, and occasional triumphs I've learned a few things about personal growth and fulfillment. I'd like to think that my own experiences and observations— together with some additional study—have provided some lessons and good practices that may help you as they have helped me. Those, together with your reflection on your own life's journey, may lead you to a better place. And that is my wish for us all.

Section 1

CHARACTER IS THE CORNERSTONE OF PERSONAL FULFILLMENT

To explore the subjects of fulfillment, success, and happiness we've got to start at their very heart—the bedrock that makes them last. We all know that where we build something, we look for a place where the ground is firm and resists erosion. We then drive a foundation into it, using material that's strong; something that can handle the pressure of the structure's weight and the elements. We ensure the base is well-constructed and held in place before we start framing.

Our lives are no different in this respect. If you're to achieve a life of personal fulfillment, whatever that may mean to you, you have to make sure it's built on a foundation that can stand the test of time. That structure has to withstand the forces of circumstance that will rain down on it, along with the howling winds of personal change. It's got to be durable. That foundation is *character*.

Author J.R. Miller wrote about character more than a century ago, saying, "The only thing that walks back from the tomb and refuses to be buried is the character of a man." Character is synonymous with legacy. It's not only something to build our lives upon; it outlasts us as well. We'll all be remembered for something when we no longer walk this earth. A life of character helps us shape what those memories of us will hold.

As is the case for many human traits, character isn't a clearly defined concept; there's no universal definition of the ingredients that comprise it. There's no recipe that all agree, when mixed and baked properly, results in a form of character that's both sweet to the taste and pleasing to the eye. Because character has both moral and intellectual components, even if we settled on the list of ingredients, how we measure and mix them would vary based on social and cultural norms and historical influences. Then there's the question of degrees: Does someone either have or lack character? Or are there subtle shades and hues?

Defining an ideal for character on the basis of these realities is certainly challenging, but I think it's important to discuss the concept of character, because if you do find yourself lacking in it (however you choose to define it), you'll find it hard to direct your life toward true fulfillment. In this section, I outline the facets I feel are important to character. You and I may have some character beliefs in common, and we may also have some different views about it. For this reason, I think it's important to ground our search for fulfillment, success, and happiness in an exploration of character.

INTEGRITY

Integrity must be discussed before the rest of the character traits because it's the beating heart of character. Character simply can't exist without integrity. Integrity is the trait that ensures you can live with yourself as you journey through life. It is your moral compass, pointing you in the direction of right and just behavior based on your sense of values and beliefs. Much like character itself, because our values and beliefs vary, there is no universal definition for integrity.

While how you perceive integrity is ultimately your choice, societies often have a large influence. For example, most would agree that lying, cheating, stealing, and deliberately harming others are actions that demonstrate a lack of integrity. Some might also agree that taking credit for others' accomplishments and shifting blame to others for your actions in order to avoid consequences are also wrong. So, it's important to note that while you may have some discretion when it comes to defining integrity based on your own values and beliefs, where your definition comes into conflict with social norms you can expect to fall afoul of others. Societies define moral boundaries in both overt ways—such as law and regulation—and more indirect ways, through exclusion from groups or negative reputations.

In order to have a sense of integrity, you must have a core set of values and beliefs. These are valuable because they not only help define north on your moral compass to point you in the direction of 'right' behavior during your life, but they also help define your identity and, in some cases, your purpose. During your life, your thoughts and actions should reflect the values and beliefs you hold.

Many people go through life feeling a sense of implied integrity based on beliefs and values they've adopted from society but have never really reflected on their individual core values and beliefs. Have you? If you haven't, take some time to ask yourself what your core values are. What do you believe in? Write them down. Review them. Word them intentionally. The more clearly you craft them for yourself and others, the more effectively you can make decisions about your life that will align with those beliefs and values.

Integrity is absolutely a prerequisite for a life with character, and a life with character is needed for true and lasting happiness, fulfillment, and achievement.

We live in an ever-increasingly interconnected world. To be human *is* to be connected to others in some way. You can't build strong, enduring relationships with others who don't trust you or who do not perceive you to be an honest and morally upstanding person. Whether this is in pursuit of love, the role of a parent, sibling, or child, or in your work profession, our happiness, success, and fulfillment—as we define it—does not occur in a human vacuum. It comes from contact with those who affect our journey.

As John Maxwell stated in *Becoming a Person of Influence*, "Integrity is your best friend. And it's also one of the best friends that your friends will ever have. When the people around you know you're a person of integrity, they know that you want to influence them because of the opportunity to add value to their lives. They don't have to worry about your motives."[1]

There's a comfort for others in knowing that your intentions are benign and that they don't have to worry about manipulation and dishonesty in your actions. They count on you, and the price of the faith they place in you is meeting their expectation of integrity. When we work together as spouses, family members, and coworkers, we depend on others to be morally upstanding to help achieve our mutual aims and preserve relationships. Even if we live our lives largely independent of others, we're unable to avoid the self-conflict, guilt, and shame of acting in a way that lacks integrity. You simply can't outrun your own mind.

You can't put a price on integrity. It's one of the few things you carry with you wherever you go in life. You can't escape it, nor its consequences, and it's mortgaged all too cheaply and regularly today. Giving it away starts with a simple decision to act in a way that doesn't fully meet our standards of integrity—things like withholding information or telling half-truths and little white lies. Emboldened by the immediate benefits and lack of consequences from the outside world, some succumb to doing it again. They lie, cheat, or steal—small things at first—and then commit more brazen acts when no one catches them. After all, who is going to know?

We do, for a start.

Integrity often dies in this manner—a death of a thousand cuts rather than some spectacular single immoral act. It's a process of erosion rather than implosion.

Eventually there may come a point when the foundation of our character becomes so weakened that we finally experience the full weight of consequences. It might be that the immoral act has come to light and you now face the world's scrutiny. It may also be that the burden becomes too much for you to bear yourself, and it starts to negatively affect your thoughts and emotions. While we all have seen examples of singular acts that loudly announce someone's moral bankruptcy to the world, often played out in the media, the death of integrity is normally a quieter, more gradual process. But one with no less severe consequences for our lives.

It's important to understand that we all have stumbles with integrity—instances when we have failed to properly reflect our values and beliefs in our thoughts and actions, or violations of some moral norm. Our discussion regarding integrity isn't to condemn anyone's past, only to acknowledge its consequences and encourage a life better aligned with integrity moving forward.

As a child, when we begin forming our beliefs and values and learning social and moral norms, we were likely got an earful from our parents and perhaps be sent to our room to think about the wrong we had done when we told a lie or cheated. As an adult, the world is far less forgiving when a lack of integrity is brought to light. The consequences are far more severe. And they should be. The harm a lack of integrity can inflict upon others grows as we grow. Our responsibility to ourselves and others increases as we age, and for that reason those lacking a moral compass are excluded in society as a form of risk management.

So, be sure to identify your values and beliefs clearly. Make sure they fundamentally align with society's moral norms. Commit to them. Use them as guidance for your thinking and behavior. Success achieved through moral shortcuts will feel hollow and fleeting. You will know it was stolen rather than earned. Achievement and happiness won in alignment with your integrity will always taste much sweeter and be more fulfilling for you. Choose the right path over the easy one.

If you are unable to commit to a life of integrity, put the book down. Nothing in the following pages will be of use to you if you aren't interested in living a moral life, one aligned with your beliefs and values. Your chances of being happy, successful, and fulfilled are slim. If you have already committed, or are willing to commit, to a moral life aligned with your beliefs and values, read on. You'll build a foundation that we can work on together as we explore the other main facets that contribute to your personal fulfillment.

HUMILITY

In a swipe-left-swipe-right world dominated by social media's friends, followers, connections, and means to live vicariously through an online persona, it's never been easier to feed the ravenous appetite of the ego. We upgrade our status and importance in the online world by gathering as many people into our flock as possible. We are virtual celebrities, manufacturing our significance via our cyber life. Pose with that new handbag or pair of shoes and boost your profile. Post every thought that pops into your head and watch as online groupies multiply. We are the center of our own virtual universe—the sun in our own sky. It's more in vogue to be self-centered than at any point in history.

Ego is the sense of self-worth and identity that our minds produce to prop up our positions of power and status, as well as our confidence. It is a fundamental part of our self-image. We all have ego, and ego is, in and of itself, not a bad phenomenon. A sound degree of self-esteem and confidence helps us feel significant. It can also support the faith in ourselves that allows us to cope with challenges to our self-worth and leads us toward achievement. Left unchecked, however, ego can quickly grow out of control and lead to an unhealthy sense of our importance, ability, and intellect that outstrips reality. That can cause some very real negative effects on both our relationships with others and our ability to realize more of our own potential.

When ego allows us to blindly believe the press our minds produce, without checks and balances, we can become arrogant and disrespectful. This stems from overvaluing ourselves and undervaluing the thoughts, feelings, and contributions of others. We begin to sincerely believe that we're always the smartest person in the room—and it shows. It shows when we stifle others' opinions or ask for them superficially before quickly dismissing them. It also shows when we judge others' opinions that run counter to our own as flawed thinking rather than try to understand them. There's no room for debate and diverse opinions in the arrogant person's orbit; they simply won't stand for it.

The unwillingness to receive feedback or reflect on the merits of others' thinking leads to isolation. Others will simply stop sharing their ideas and opinions when it's wasted time for all involved. You're then left to cope with life's challenges and setbacks completely on your own. In doing so, you've squandered the goodwill and potential of others to help you along the journey, which is most unfortunate.

The willingness to receive and act on feedback is one of the most valuable tools for increasing your self-awareness and managing both your relationships and situational outcomes. If you allow ego to put blinders on you, you produce your own obstacles on the way to happiness and fulfillment.

There's a saying originally from the Bible that goes: *pride cometh before the fall*. All this really means is that your ego causes a fall from grace. If you've ever known an egotist or narcissist with a clearly overblown sense of self-worth, their behaviors—even if they temporarily lead them up the ladder of success—always serve to eventually topple them off the pedestal they put themselves on. Being an egotist or narcissist is simply not a sustainable way of living.

Humility is a wonderful personal resource that guards against these perils. An overabundance of ego repels people and makes relationship-building difficult. Humility often has the opposite effect. Others are drawn to people who are grounded enough to demonstrate modest behaviors. We're attracted to such people because they readily demonstrate the respect and value for others that all of us desire.

To cultivate humility, listen to others and take their viewpoints into account. They'll continue to share great ideas and counsel that will help you make wise decisions and avoid disaster when you close your mouth and open your ears. The basic respect that considerate listening shows others will help you achieve more because you have now accessed collective brainpower rather than relying solely on your own. Doing so also allows others to be truly heard, which satisfies a basic human need for significance.

Bring realism to your assessment of your flaws and limitations. We all have them, whether we like to admit it or not. Anyone who fails to acknowledge their flaws and limitations deludes only themselves, as others can see them regardless. The humble person doesn't dwell incessantly on them, but does seek out areas they can be better as an initial step toward personal growth.

In addition, acknowledge your limitations. It will keep you from letting pride and ego get in the way of asking for help and seeking counsel when needed. It is a shame to fail alone when a helping hand is sitting close by, just waiting for you to ask.

Admit to your mistakes and apologize. Others can see when you make them anyways, and pridefully denying that reality only damages relationships. Own the problems you create and the mistakes you make and apologize when your actions have harmed others. We all know the value of a sincere apology. It acknowledges your harmful words or actions and your willingness to be accountable for their consequences.

There's a Chinese proverb that says: "Be like the bamboo. The higher you grow, the deeper you bow." This is humility in action. Share credit for accomplishments with others whenever you can. Achievement is rarely a solitary affair, and we usually have others to thank for contributing along the way. Sharing credit demonstrates basic respect and includes others in the feel-good narrative of your success story.

In addition, express gratitude for others, including the personal traits that you admire. The egotist has a thirst that can never be quenched, always concentrating on what they don't have rather than expressing thanks for what they do. Humility isn't the opposite of ambition, but it does cause us to pause and reflect on our good fortune in life—even when current circumstances are difficult.

The humble person sees special and valuable qualities in others, even if they aren't obvious. They understand that everyone is an expert at something and we can learn from one another. The humble person's learning journey is never finished, which is why they unlock more of their potential than the egotist. While the pool of the egotist is superficial and shallow, the humble person's is deep with substance.

The modest person also isn't an obsessive self-promoter, which can be out of place in today's look-at-me-I'm-special world of tweets, online posts, blogs, and social media. While there's nothing wrong with occasionally reminding yourself or others of the progress you've made, there's a difference between simple acknowledgment and the constant attention-seeking of egotists. Talk is cheap; let your actions speak for you instead. Quietly do your best in any endeavor and you'll reward yourself through your conscientiousness. If others recognize your success, that's great. If not, it doesn't detract from your accomplishments. (Although, it's nice to be appreciated. If you are habitually ignored by others, it might be time to find a new environment that allows you to openly shine).

So, guard yourself against self-love and an excess of ego. There's a good reason Emperor Marcus Aurelius had someone constantly follow him, whispering "you're just a man" whenever a citizen of Rome bowed before him. This servant was humility personified, and you have the same ability to keep your ego in check through humble self-dialogue.

- *Are you honest and transparent about your intentions with others, or do you sometimes lie, cheat, or steal to get what you want in life?*
- *Do you do the right things and make hard decisions in order to protect your integrity and the welfare of others?*
- *Does your ego sometimes cause you to act disrespectfully or lead you to believe that you're better than others?*
- *Do you demonstrate humility by being open to learning from others and taking their opinions into account?*
- *Can you admit to yourself and others when you've made mistakes or behaved badly?*

ACCOUNTABILITY

Accountability occupies a special place in the concept of character, as well as in work and life. It's a key factor for success and a critical part of any endeavor. Accountability lies at the very heart of the philosophy that success is borne from understanding expectations, owning results, and following up. Working toward fulfillment and success in your life means taking ownership of your thoughts, actions, and outcomes—whether they are good or bad.

It should be no surprise that accountability has many definitions. I believe one of the best definitions of accountability is simply *doing what you said you'd do, when and how you said you'd do it.* When this happens, you close the gap between talk and action, as well as between others' perceptions of you and how you *want* them to view you. You no longer have to worry about image management, because your accountability handles that for you.

When you consistently deliver on your word, your reputation takes care of itself.

But there's a challenge with accountability that modern societies demonstrate. It's become more common and acceptable to view ourselves as passengers in our own lives, with our actions and their consequences seen as the result of outside influences rather the product of our own choices. It seems the world at large is to blame for our problems, and it's fashionable to deny our part in the circumstances of our lives. Personal accountability has been badly eroded as a result. As personal accountability experts Roger Connors, Tom Smith, and Craig Hickman put it in *The Oz Principle*:

> Pop psychology, whether intentional or not, has often encouraged people in our society to blame all their woes and problems on a single or few experiences in their lives, thus promoting a lack of accountability for current and future behaviors, attitudes, and feelings … Blaming everything on their past wounds, they explain their vulnerability to fad diets, their awkwardness in relating to children, or their feelings of alienation and loneliness, as if no other modern adult suffers these problems. The fact is, whether you are a true victim or a pseudovictim, you will never overcome a hurtful past until you develop a present- and future-oriented view of your own accountability for getting more out of life.[2]

In other words, until we look in the mirror rather than pointing a finger outward, none of us will make meaningful progress in owning the current circumstances of our lives and acting to improve them. Just like the first step to curing any addiction is to acknowledge its existence, we can't move away from a victim mentality that denies personal responsibility until we're aware that it exists in the first place. You have to see that the victim mentality is there and own it in order to put victimization in the rearview mirror. You are the primary influencer of the direction of your life and the manner in which you want it to play out. You can relinquish that power to outside forces, but even that is still your choice.

We all fall into the trap of telling ourselves that we're the victims, others are the cause of our problems, and we are powerless to change the narrative. But there's an important difference between the occasional visitor to Victimville and those who choose to reside there. Make sure that you don't live your own life vicariously through the role of perpetual victim. Cast off the passenger mentality and captain your life's direction. No one else is qualified to take the helm, and the journey will never be as fulfilling when someone else steers the ship. It's perfectly okay to have navigators along for the ride from time to time. These are people who coach, counsel, and support you. But we all know that there's a fundamental difference between driver and passenger. When you take accountability for the happenings of your life, successes taste so much sweeter and setbacks become learning experiences—and both are valuable to you in the long term.

When you consistently practice accountability, you also increase your value to others. Those who follow through on commitments, own their mistakes, demonstrate conscientiousness and tenacity to deliver on their word, and seek help in order to accomplish goals are cherished by others. We understand that such people can be trusted; they are reliable and will support themselves and others well. In the workplace, these qualities are often lauded, which is a subject Mark Samuel eloquently discusses in *Making Yourself Indispensable*.[3]

In order to develop accountability, be specific about your commitments. Whether you determine expectations yourself or they are set for you, you need to have clarity so that you can fulfill them. At work, you ask your boss when needed to ensure you understand expectations. In the rest of your life, you often create this clarity for yourself or talk with others if the accountability is within a relationship. Accountable people make simple and precise commitments so that others can assess whether those commitments have been successfully met.

Accountability also provides focus and direction to our lives that keeps us from wandering aimlessly down roads that lead to nowhere. Vague expectations for yourself are a form of victim mentality when you allow yourself to rationalize meeting a goal that was always written in pencil rather than carved in stone. Tentative, vague goals signal a lack of accountability and will damage your credibility in the eyes of others. Remember, when you make commitments to others, accountability is in the eyes of the beholder. What is most important isn't whether *you* believe you followed through on your word; it's whether *others* believe you've done so. Being specific provides a clearer picture for all parties to measure accountability against.

Feedback also helps you increase and sustain your accountability. Seek it out and be appreciative when others take the time to provide it. Feedback helps you understand the gap between how you perceive your follow-through on commitments and how others view it. The harsh reality is that no one really cares if *you* think you've done a great job with accountability. Others are the ultimate judge of your ability to keep your word. In a world where talk is cheap and plentiful, those who consistently "walk the walk" have become rare jewels. You'll gain fans because of your ability to be accountable for your actions and results, including your mistakes. Feedback is particularly useful when failures occur. It may sting a bit, but learning about your shortcomings keeps you humble and correcting them helps you better deliver on future commitments and meet expectations.

Follow-up and self-audits play important roles in supporting accountability. When you take the time to periodically inspect what you expect of yourself, you're able to assess progress in keeping your commitments and alter your behaviors to increase the chances that you will deliver on them. Build regular self-audits into any commitment you make—to yourself or others—so that you can consistently be a person of your word. Remember, too, that when you follow up with others to ensure that you delivered as you said you would, you gain the ability to correct any mistakes and build goodwill along the way. When others follow up with you, as is common in the workplace, remember that they usually have everyone's best interests at heart. Don't view this as an annoyance or intrusion. Your boss or coworker wants to see you succeed just as much as you do. You all have a vested interest in a positive outcome, after all.

So, accountability is a key character trait that supports success in any of life's pursuits. Keeping commitments to yourself and others is a virtue that builds your personal credibility and is the bedrock of performance. This is why accountable individuals and teams perform consistently and fulfill more of their potential—and build self-esteem along the way. Keeping our word consistently makes us feel good about ourselves, which is important to our long-term happiness.

In *The Fred Factor*, leadership strategist Mark Sanborn asks the following thought-provoking questions about accountability for you to consider: "Think about it. Do you add to or take away from the experience of your customers and colleagues? Do you move your organization closer to or further from its goals? Do you perform your work in an ordinary way, or do you execute it superbly? Do you lighten someone's burden or add to it? Do you lift someone up or put someone down? *Nobody can prevent you from choosing to be exceptional.*"4

COMPASSION AND FORGIVENESS

If we are to succeed in being human, we must demonstrate the most human character traits: showing care, kindness, and concern, and forgiving both ourselves and others for transgressions.

We can't journey through life expecting others to be concerned for our welfare if we don't also care for—and empathize with—them. Can we really *feel* the pain and distress that relationship breakups, serious health issues, career setbacks, and the deaths of those close to others cause them, or do we just pay them lip service? Do we make a sincere effort to support others during their times of greatest need—helping them, validating them, listening, and providing wise counsel? The ability to identify with others' problems and pain—and taking action to alleviate them—is the heart of compassion, along with actions to celebrate others' triumphs and joys. Compassion is a basic expectation of human decency, and it is necessary to build strong and lasting relationships with others.

We've all run across others who are cold and unfeeling, who treat other people as a means to an end. They are superficial and connect with others only to use them for their own purposes. This manipulation is commonplace, which is very unfortunate. The nature of relationships is give-and-take, and when people treat interactions like a business transaction it cheapens the human experience. They also miss the real point of life, which is to live it. You can't truly be alive when you treat others like a commodity and take emotion out of the equation. The nothing-personal-it's-just-business approach to interacting with others grows old quickly. When others come to realize they're being manipulated and taken advantage of, you'll end up with few friends and little respect. No one likes a heartless jerk, after all.

Little things matter. Everything we do sends a signal to others about our character, priorities, and values. A word of encouragement to support others in tough times—like being there to lend a sympathetic ear and listen to a friend's problems, or expressing our condolences in times of personal loss—are all ways to show others that we care. People are likely draw the opposite conclusion if you overlook them. Supportive conversations lift others up in dark times and are a blessing to them, while a few venomous words can erode self-esteem, cause unnecessary conflict, and can destroy others emotionally.

Compassion is a remarkable personal resource. Demonstrating care and concern for others makes them feel good. We all take comfort when we know that we're not alone in this world and that someone else thinks kindly of us. Knowing that others are looking out for our welfare is a warm emotional blanket we wrap ourselves in. When others need the same empathy and reassurance, we would do well to remember how impactful it can be and provide it for them in turn.

We can't really cherish the emotional triumphs in life until we've experienced tragedy. Whether the triumphs are our own or someone else's is irrelevant. Compassion allows us to live vicariously through others and brings richness to the human experience. Compassion allows us to experience joy, love, and achievement and multiplies our good feeling. We also experience tragedy, pain, and failure through others. But this is the depth of feeling that stirs our souls and reminds us we're alive. Would you rather live half a life, full of mild contentment and minor setbacks, or experience moments of overwhelming joy and acute pain? I choose the latter every time, because I only get to live this life once and I don't want to experience it in half measures.

It's important to remember that compassion isn't just for others; it's for yourself too. Living in the land of self-recrimination and regret is no fun. Many people languish there, eroding their own self-esteem and generating a sense of hopelessness. Don't do this to yourself. There's an important difference between taking the time to analyze and reflect on what went wrong in order to gain wisdom and obsessively ruminating over the problems in your life. You're going to make mistakes, fail, embarrass yourself, and experience tragedy. You can't escape it; it's part of life. You can, however, decide whether to take the lessons learned from these experiences and move on. You must face forward without looking over your shoulder if you're to successfully reach life's next destination. Give yourself a break. In order to completely love yourself, you have to embrace your flaws and failures as well as your strengths and successes and extend yourself the same compassion you would expect from others.

Another aspect of character important to joy and fulfillment is forgiveness. We know the emotional relief when others extend forgiveness for a wrong we committed. Forgiveness helps wash away the dark atmosphere that exists between people. It wipes the slate clean in our psyche and allows the damage to a relationship to more quickly heal. A grudge is like a festering wound that never heals. A sackful of animosity, resentment, and bitterness becomes heavy over time and infects other areas of our life. Antipathy greedily burns through precious emotional resources that could be redirected toward pursuits that support our happiness and fulfillment instead.

Forgiveness is often mistakenly seen as only being of value to others, but the beneficiaries of forgiveness are *both* the giver and receiver. The receiver gains absolution for their wrongs, and the giver also benefits greatly and can finally set down their burden of animosity, resentment, and bitterness—an unnecessary part of life's experience to begin with.

In *Making Yourself Indispensable*, Mark Samuel says, "The purpose of forgiveness is to let go of the baggage you don't need. The point here is not to address whether you were right, whether the other person should be punished, or whether he or she deserves to be forgiven. Each person has his or her unique value system, and it would be impossible to address all of them here. What matters is that forgiveness is done for your own benefit."[5] Whether consciously or unconsciously, we always act on our strong feelings. Forgiveness allows you to change your focus from the past—and negativity—to a more positive outlook for the journey ahead.

- *Do you demonstrate accountability by following through on your commitments—doing what you said you'd do, when and how you said you'd do it?*
- *Do you take responsibility for mistakes and bad behavior? Do you own the results of your actions, apologizing and correcting them when they negatively affect others?*
- *Do you demonstrate compassion and kindness?*
- *Can you empathize with others' problems and pain? Do you take steps to help lift them up whenever you can?*
- *Do you demonstrate forgiveness, or do you have a critical heart?*

Section 2
EMOTIONAL INTELLIGENCE

N ext to the bedrock foundation of character, the connections and authenticity that underpin fulfillment lie within the competency of *emotional intelligence*. This sits at the right hand of character because of the crucial partnership between emotional intelligence and character that supports achievement and healthy relationships with ourselves and others. The ability to identify, comprehend, and handle both our own feelings and those of others is emotional intelligence in action. Emotional intelligence allows us to influence our thoughts and actions—and those of others—in ways that support our (ethical) aspirations and goals. It is intra- and interpersonal expertise that separates those who seem to cruise gracefully through encounters and the storms of their lives from those who flounder near the rocky shores. In his seminal book *Emotional Intelligence*, Daniel Goleman says of self-mastery:

> A sense of self-mastery, of being able to withstand the emotional storms that the buffeting of Fortune brings rather than being "passion's slave," has been praised as a virtue since the time of Plato. The ancient Greek

word for it was *sophrosyne*, "care and intelligence in conducting one's life; a tempered balance and wisdom" … The goal is balance, not emotional suppression: every feeling has its value and significance. A life without passion would be a dull wasteland of neutrality, cut off and isolated from the richness of life itself. But, as Aristotle observed, what is wanted is *appropriate* emotion, feeling proportionate to circumstance.[6]

We may more commonly—and mistakenly—identify such a quality as 'social skills,' which are within the realm of emotional intelligence but are not the same. There's no doubt, however, that we all have experience with those who have high emotional intelligence and were likely left with envy, admiration, or respect for the bearer of good emotional awareness and control. Emotional intelligence is an important meta-competency that preempts credibility, rapport, relationship management, and considered decision-making. It is likely to be *the* pivotal factor in your self-fulfillment and achievement.

As Price Pritchett points out in *Hard Optimism*, performance begins in our head, and in today's knowledge economy, it stays there.[7] The tool for productive behavior has shifted from the hands and feet of the labor economy to the mind because it's the quality of thought that determines outcomes in the postmodern world. What has always been true at home is now also true in the workplace; understanding our emotional being and using that knowledge to positively influence our own—and others'—lives is a critical competency.

At home, emotional intelligence affects the quality of marriage and our relationships with friends, relatives, and those we encounter in our daily lives—just as it has always done. Now the central importance of emotional intelligence at work has also been recognized as global economies have shifted from blue to white collar, from labor-intensive manufacturing to technology and services, and from steady and predictable to fast-paced innovation and change. The emotional qualities that have long made for good spouses, friends, and neighbors now make for good bosses and teammates as well.

We all have witnessed acts of low emotional intelligence (EQ) (or committed them ourselves at some point, which makes us perfectly normal) and the damage they cause. The friend or coworker who succumbs to a fit of rage, reacting in a way that damages relationships and their own credibility in the process. The boss or relative who shows no empathy for others, treating people like numbers and failing to demonstrate care and compassion when it's most needed. The significant other who is unable to control their anxiety and attitude, continuously ruminating over the past or future and viewing it through a negative lens.

You've probably also noticed that EQ is independent of IQ; raw intellect has no real bearing on someone's level of emotional intelligence. Petulant, frustrated geniuses prone to tantrums or oblivious to the feelings of others abound, wondering why they underachieve in relation to their potential and alienate those they encounter. With their nose too often in a book or in front of the computer screen, such people aren't in tune with their own or others' thoughts and feelings. In a world where few activities and achievements are solitary affairs, true fulfillment and success fall out of reach for those individuals. Groundbreaking theorist Daniel Goleman, in *Emotional Intelligence*, aptly described the inability of educational systems to develop emotional intelligence, stating:

> …academic intelligence offers virtually no preparation for the turmoil— or opportunity—life's vicissitudes bring … Emotional life is a domain that, as surely as math or reading, can be handled with greater or lesser skills, and requires a unique set of competencies. And how adept a person is at those is crucial to understanding why one person thrives in life while another, of equal intellect, dead-ends: emotional aptitude is a *meta-ability*, determining how well we can use whatever other skills we have, including raw intellect.[8]

Goleman's assertion is supported by Eric Jordan in *Emotional Intelligence Mastery*, who references a study at the University of California in Berkeley that spanned over forty years. The study focused on PhD-level professionals and concluded that having well-developed emotional intelligence was four times more powerful than IQ in predicting who would succeed in their respective chosen fields.[9] Numerous research studies since have found emotional intelligence to be beneficial for success, relationships, self-fulfillment, and happiness.

Whether you're a PhD or an executive at the top of your chosen profession (or one of us more ordinary people looking to build a foundation for fulfillment and healthy relationships), the critical supporting role of emotional mastery is undeniable. There are several interdependent factors of emotional intelligence and understanding them will help you greatly as you explore other important personal competencies—such as resilience and stress tolerance, self-development, performance management, and accountability.

SELF-AWARENESS

We have to wait too long in a line at the bank, in traffic, or on the phone with the utility company. Our blood begins to boil and we spontaneously bark rudely at those around us, displaying our clear displeasure. An initial setback or rejection occurs, and we instantly read it as a sign of our own enduring inadequacies and prediction of future failures. A spiral of anxiety and depression ensues. Our ideas or sphere of authority is challenged; we quickly and angrily lash out at the perceived offender or send a poison-pen email to document our feelings toward them.

Each of us has experienced events or circumstances that move us to rapid and unthinking emotional reaction—one which may be extreme and, when the waters calm, we find regrettable. You've likely heard the term "hindsight is 20/20," meaning that with the benefits of time and emotional distance, we're able to more clearly see the thoughts and actions that would have been more constructive. If we're to control our emotions and influence thoughts and actions, we've got to understand ourselves—both from our own point of view and that of others. Self-awareness is a simple concept but one that is hard to describe and implement. Tasha Eurich describes self-awareness as being two-pronged in her excellent book *Insight*:

Internal self-awareness has to do with seeing yourself clearly. It's an inward understanding of your values, passions, aspirations, ideal environment, patterns, reactions, and impact on others. People who are high in internal self-awareness tend to make choices that are consistent with who they really are, allowing them to lead happier and more satisfying lives ... *External self-awareness* is about understanding yourself from the outside in—that is, **knowing how other people see you**. Because externally self-aware people can accurately see themselves from others' perspectives, they are able to builder stronger and more trusting relationships.[10] (P. 8)

Eurich describes self-awareness as a meta-skill, one which cuts across many facets of communication and relationship management in our lives. To be sure, we can't improve the way we think, feel, and act from a state of personal ignorance. Improvement requires a starting point; a benchmark from which to assess our progress and results. Without this knowledge, we remain unaware of our challenges controlling ourselves, the situations that evoke the strongest reactions, and the direction in which we need to turn when unhealthy thoughts and feelings well up. It would be like having a map without any knowledge of where you are. It's useless.

Self-awareness is the GPS of our emotional lives; it tells us where we are by cross-referencing our awareness of ourselves (emotional longitude) and the perspectives of others (emotional latitude) to help us pinpoint our current emotional location. Without it, we're left gazing at the landscape and landmarks using a warped view—one which is rarely correct and does not lead us down the path to personal fulfillment.

The damage of self-ignorance isn't just conceptual. In *Insight*, Eurich references research that indicates the negative impact of self-ignorance both at home and in the workplace. She asserts that lack of self-awareness reduces decision quality by about 36 percent and cooperation by 46 percent, as well as increasing conflict by 30 percent. Companies with large numbers of self-ignorant staff were 79 percent more likely to have poor financial returns. At home, self-ignorance and bullish views of personality and behavior were seen to be the cause of one out of four emotionally distant relationships.[11]

The self-aware you, having achieved an improved level of understanding via introspection, is keenly interested in the thoughts and opinions of others, including the feedback you can glean about yourself. By taking a deep and genuine interest in others, you gain greater insight about your abilities, values, fears, aspirations, and motivations—all of which are important for building healthy relationships, cooperation, and influence. The ability to focus on others signals respect, concern, value, and support for them—all of which positively impact the quality of relationships. There is little doubt that self-awareness is a prerequisite master skill for fulfillment and success more than ever before.

INTERNAL SELF-AWARENESS

Our awareness of our thoughts, emotions, and resulting behaviors is a critical condition for self-control, as well as the creation of choice in our actions. We often fail to notice that, in the words of John Milton, "The mind is its own place, and can itself make a heaven out of hell, a hell out of heaven …" The threads of our thoughts, feelings, hopes, fears, dreams, and drivers are woven together to form the rich tapestry of our lives. Our interpretation of the events we experience creates our reality. The lives we lead lie within the vast space between our two ears—not out in the world somewhere.

If our world, then, and the lives we lead are the products of our own unique sense of reality, we must come to know ourselves better if we're to shape and control our lives. The events that occur or our circumstances aren't 'good' or 'bad'; they just *are*. Only our interpretation paints them with subjective value, which is why some people see crisis and tragedy when others see opportunity and rebirth. Ian Tuhovky also asserted this in his book *Emotional Intelligence*: the power of choice you have in how you interpret situations means you also have choices regarding your resulting emotional state.[12]

While this sounds easy in theory, many of us are either unaware of our power to mold our interpretations in ways which serve us better or fail to become self-aware enough to exert meaningful control over our interpretations and thoughts—which result in our feelings and behavior. Susan David describes this challenge eloquently in *Emotional Agility*:

This voice of consciousness is a silent but tireless chatterbox, secretly barraging us with observations, comments, and analyses without pause.

Moreover, this ceaseless internal voice is what literature professors call an unreliable narrator ... While we often accept these statements bubbling up from within this river of incessant chatter as being factual, most are a complex mixture of evaluations and judgments, intensified by our emotions. Some of these thoughts are positive and helpful; others are negative and unhelpful. In either case our inner voice is rarely neutral or dispassionate.[13]

We are both the convincing salesman and gullible consumer of interpretation in our lives, rarely stopping to question the facts and evidence we present to ourselves. We ruminate over disproportion, warped perspective, negative worldviews, 'bad' intention, and victim statements, seldom pausing to acknowledge the existence of alternative interpretations. Internal self-awareness asks us to do just that: to put space between the event, our interpretation of it, and the emotions that result from them and fill that space with a more detached, dispassionate view that serves us better.

The first step in this process is to admit two fundamental realities. This first is that we are a relative stranger to ourselves and in need of a proper introduction. The second is that, even when we form a much closer relationship with ourselves and become internally self-aware, we are still relatively poor judges of ourselves. We still need to color our view with others' perspectives of us in order to form a coherent sense of self-awareness.

INTERNAL SELF-AWARENESS AND CORE VALUES

To understand your interpretations, thoughts, and feelings better and become more internally self-aware, you have to explore the lenses through which you view the world. There are some foundational aspects of yourself that influence your perspectives, patterns of thought, and feelings. By identifying and exploring these, you'll not only increase your understanding of yourself but also use them as compass points by which to navigate more effectively toward personal fulfillment and happiness. Identifying and understanding your core values is the first step in this process, because without them our lives feel like we are at sea without a sail to capture the wind or a compass to guide our journey. As Susan David puts it in *Emotional Agility*:

> To make decisions that match up with the way you hope to live, you have to be in touch with the things that matter to you so you can use them as signposts. If you've never taken the time to sort out your values, then you're always winging it, which is how we end up frittering away our time ... Making choices and negotiating relationships without a clear set of governing values at the front of your mind is exhausting. It involves not only the confusing work of facing the world each day with everything up for grabs, but sometimes it means retrofitting your emotions so they appear to line up with what you think is expected of you ...[14]

Your core values are a crucial lens through which you view and interpret the world. In fact, the word *evaluate* has its origins in *value* and is defined in part as the process of determining something's worth or priority. It *is* the process of interpretation based upon the principles you've defined as important markers by which to judge actions and events as either 'good' or 'bad,' valuable or worthless. They are also aspirational, and you can assess your progress on the journey to becoming who you want to be by referring back to these principles for living. We don't judge every happening, but those that intersect with our core values are bound to evoke a reaction. When the two collide at full speed, the reaction can be strong.

I've asked participants in my leadership training to identify and write down their core values. The exercise is a lot harder than it sounds, because very few of us have consciously thought about and documented our most deeply held principles. We know they exist, but we trust that they'll surface and instinctively guide us like some invisible hand rather than act to consciously influence our action. We also need to go beyond just identifying our core values in order to become meaningfully self-aware. We've got to explore *why* we hold those principles so dear.

- *What are things you believe strongly that have guided your thoughts and actions?*
- *Do you use those beliefs to evaluate 'right' and 'wrong,' 'good' and 'bad,' or 'valuable' and 'worthless'?*
- *Are these beliefs long-standing? Have they endured over the years?*

Write down the important principles/beliefs that you identify as your core values.

- *Think about the important or influential events in your life. How have they been connected to your core values?*
- *When an event occurs that intersects with one of your core values, do you notice a strong emotional reaction?*
- *Why are each of these principles/beliefs so important to you? What is it about each, and how it has interacted with your life, that makes it so dear to you?*

Hopefully this exercise allows you to identify and understand what is important to you and why. This is pivotal for increasing your self-awareness and providing focus to your life that can increase your fulfillment. Without focus, everything becomes important—and if everything is important, then nothing is. That is when we find ourselves directionless. As Ryan Holiday aptly put it in *Ego is the Enemy*, "It's time to sit down and think about what's truly important to you and then take steps to forsake the rest. Without this, success will not be pleasurable, or nearly as complete as it could be. Or worse, it won't last."[15]

So, your core values ground you when the sands of change begin shifting under your feet or you encounter unfamiliar situations. You can interpret the happenings of your life through the lens of whether they're aligned with your core values or run counter to them. This allows you to make decisions consistent with your closely held beliefs. Your actions become more authentic representations of who you really are and who you aspire to be—and that can be absolutely liberating.

INTERNAL SELF-AWARENESS AND OUR ASPIRATIONS AND MOTIVATORS

We need to identify and understand our dreams and drivers to increase self-awareness. These may be related to or stem from our core principles, but are not the same as them. Our aspirations are the important, long-term aims for our lives. They are not goals, which are finite things to be achieved and then set on the shelf somewhere (e.g., buy a house, become a director in my firm, run my first marathon).

Aspirations are enduring and deeply held desires for our lives that we continually strive for (e.g., positively impact others throughout my life by educating them about leadership and personal fulfillment, continually learn and grow personally and professionally by increasing my emotional intelligence, contribute to health and wellbeing in my communities through my words and actions). They are destinations we may grow closer to during the course of our lives, but they can never actually be reached. Because of this, they have an intimate connection to meaning and motivation. Aspirations are like icebreakers at sea in winter; they encounter adversity, resistance, and harsh conditions but have the ability to keep us moving forward by finding ways to shift seemingly immovable objects. In this way, they are also tied to the concept of resilience.

This isn't to say that goals are unimportant or meaningless. They may or may not support our aspirations and are typically finite, short-term aims. They don't provide a deep sense of meaning to our lives in and of themselves. Think of your aspirations like a form of renewable energy—wind, sun, or water. They can continually be harnessed to provide emotional energy for our lives, helping move us forward even when the conditions of the day are difficult. Goals, on the other hand, provide us with batteries; they can provide us strong and temporary drive, but they eventually run out (sometimes even before the goal itself is reached). It's important that we understand both our enduring aspirations and our current, changing goals to get to know ourselves even better.

- *What are the ongoing aims for your life?*
- *Are these aims enduring? Have they remained largely unchanged over the course of at least several years?*
- *Are these aims destinations that you can strive for but never fully reach?*
- *Are these aims deeply meaningful to you in some way, possibly connected to your core values?*

These are your aspirations.

- *Do you have shorter-term objectives for your life that are more likely to be measured in months or perhaps a couple of years?*
- *Do they have an end point, some way of determining achievement with certainty?*
- *Are they likely to have less meaning and importance for you once they are reached?*
- *Do they possibly support your enduring aspirations (they don't have to, but it is good self-awareness to recognize whether they do)?*

These are your goals.

By identifying and exploring your aspirations and goals—both separately and understanding the relationship between them—you're more likely to understand which things are important to you today and which are likely to remain so for many years to come. It helps us place them in perspective and understand which are the load-bearing columns of our emotional castles and which are less crucial support beams. Put too much weight on the beams and not enough attention on identifying and using the columns and the entire structure weakens.

I've always maintained that we are all captains of our own ships. You may or may not have a crew to support you at home or in the workplace, and the ship can look more like a small sailboat at times. Nonetheless, it's ours to command as we wish—inviting others aboard and allowing them to help when conditions call for it, enjoying the ride when the sailing is easier. We must watch out for others' boats, too, tacking when needed to avoid a crash. The more we know about what drives us to get onto the water in the first place and develop our captaining skills, the better we can navigate today's waters without a nasty accident. That's the factor of *motivation*, which we also must identify and understand in ourselves.

Motivations have many facets. They can lie within you or outside of you and be either unique to you or in common with others. Don't assume that you know what *drives* your thoughts, feelings, and behaviors well. That is a skill often related to general self-awareness, which most people don't have well-developed. You also shouldn't believe that you—and only you—know your motivators. You may be operating on your shadow beliefs rather than the observed communication and behaviors that others see as your drivers. (We'll explore the subject of *external self-awareness* more later.)

THE MOTIVATORS THAT LIE OUTSIDE YOU

External drivers are often the most visible and easiest to identify, but they are also the most at risk. Rather than lying within your own heart and mind, they are somewhere 'out there' in the environment. External drivers are the things that must be given to you rather than things you give yourself. And if they are given, they can be withheld. Even when well-intentioned others mean to provide you the external driver that you desire, circumstance and those who are less benevolent may get in the way to prevent this from occurring. You may also fail to perform the needed actions in order to earn this motivator or reward that often comes when goals are reached.

When life, self-worth, identity, meaning, and happiness are defined primarily by the things that may or may not be given to you, you're constantly at risk. You're in a vulnerable state where the danger of unfulfillment constantly lurks in the shadows, which can cause perpetual anxiety and stress. For this reason, it's important to think about the place external motivators have in your life.

This is not to say that external motivators can't or shouldn't be of some value to you, but overreliance on them can be unhealthy. Ultimately, external motivators are commodities; if you can't get them in one place, you can get them somewhere else. Money, for instance, is the ultimate commodity and a common external motivator. It helps you pay for life's necessities, meet your financial obligations, and buy things in order to pursue your interests. To the degree you're motivated by these things, the motivation for money arrives by proxy. When you don't find enough of it in one place—to the degree that it motivates you above other drivers and your situation demands more money—you go looking for it in another (e.g., finding new career opportunities).

In addition to being an external motivator, *money* is a motivator offering decreasing returns. Beyond the point that it provides for your needs, offers you opportunities to pursue your life interests, and allows you to buy a few wants, it offers less and less motivation as you accumulate more of it. This is a unique point for each of us in our financial lives, of course. Our early belief that money really does buy happiness is challenged as we accumulate the stuff of our lives. We find that having obtained the material things we set out to, there's little increase in happiness than when life appeared to be simpler (and sometimes more unhappiness instead).

Money is saved, invested, and grown when we have more than we need to sustain our daily lives, but it holds less and less meaning the more and more common it becomes to us. It's the law of external motivation supply and demand: the more of something we accumulate, the less precious it becomes.

Money, too, is subject to circumstance and can be withheld from us. As I am writing this, the world is engulfed in the greatest health pandemic in a century. Not since the influenza pandemic of 1918 has there been an outbreak as severe, and none has been more impactful in terms of its effect on the global economy. Millions of jobs have been lost, millions of bonuses won't be paid, and millions of paychecks won't increase annually the way we expected them to. Your financial state may have been personally impacted by this crisis. If not, you undoubtedly know someone's who was.

Economic cycles transform and crises appear. Natural disasters occur. The political climate shifts. Leadership in companies make bad decisions that drive organizations into the ground. Mergers and acquisitions cause corporate rightsizing. New technologies make jobs obsolete. Workforce trends make talent pools for certain jobs more common—and decrease pay as a result. Consumer trends shift preferences away from products and services your employer provides (e.g., Sony Walkman, Kodak film cameras, Blockbuster Video). The boss evaluates your performance negatively and you miss out on the bonus and raise you were expecting.

You and I could come up with a hundred more situations that cause loss of income, job, or earning capacity. Money comes, and money can also go. Define your sense of identity, self-worth, and happiness by the size of your financial portfolio and you're constantly at risk to forces outside of your control. This isn't to say that money is evil at all. However, like all external motivators it's subject to forces outside of our control by its very nature. That means there's always a chance that you may never receive it as you'd hoped.

Recognition and reward are also external motivators. Praise from others, any form of reward that you value, threat of punishment or consequence, job title, promotion, and the plaque presented to you are all common external motivators designed to encourage certain behaviors or performance.

There are certain motivators that have both internal and external characteristics. These are intangible but must still be provided to you by others at times in order to support motivation. These are concepts like recognition, appreciation, encouragement, autonomy, responsibility, authority, and empowerment. Like money, these external motivators are normally given to you after you've obtained certain goals or achieved expected levels of performance. Most come *upon completion* of the activity and are not provided to you *as part of performing the activity itself.* That distinction is what separates internal from external motivators.

- *What are your strongest external motivators?*
- *What part does money play as a motivator in your life?*
- *How heavily do you rely on external motivators today to affirm your worth and maintain your self-esteem?*

THE MOTIVATORS THAT LIE WITHIN YOU

Internal motivators are drivers that come from performing an activity itself rather than being given once it's completed. The activity is intrinsically rewarding and that drives us from within to continue on.

There's greater potential for internal motivation to sustain itself over time, and the risks associated with changing environmental conditions are less because the driver lies within us. Several common types of internal motivators exist. Understand them to help you become more aware of what drives your thoughts, feelings, and behavior.

Purpose, meaning, and significance comprise one type of internal motivator. We all want to know that our lives have a purpose. Identifying and moving in the direction of it can be motivating, particularly when that purpose is connected to something beyond material wealth. When your purpose is connected to positively impacting the environment, the communities in which you live, those you encounter, or humanity in general, you have a higher purpose that transcends your self-interest and contributes to the greater good. That can be a very powerful force for action in your life.

Having an identified purpose can also increase your fulfillment, self-esteem, and sense of pride in your actions. This is recognized in many of life's pursuits, from the workplace to sports, academics, politics, and local community activities. There's an increasing emphasis on ensuring that activity is connected to higher purpose so that people can positively identify with the groups to which they belong and the way they spend their time and energy. This is why there's increasing exposure to civil rights, equality, diversity, inclusion, environmental awareness, community involvement, child welfare, and other issues as a part of our daily lives.

Only a couple of generations ago, these issues were given less overt exposure and weren't a significant part of the way we evaluated our association with others, especially our employers. Today, we're much more apt to research and evaluate career opportunities based on whether we want to be associated with our employers due to the perceived meaningfulness of their purpose. As Harter and Wagner stated in *12: The Elements of Great Managing*, "… a uniquely human twist occurs after the basic needs are fulfilled. The employee searches for meaning in her vocation. For reasons that transcend the physical needs fulfilled by earning a living, she looks for her contribution to a higher purpose. Something within her looks for something in which to believe."[16]

Closely associated with purpose are meaning and significance—the feeling that you matter and that others (e.g., people, the environment, living creatures, communities) benefit from your work and your existence. This is legacy, and the motivation to leave a positive impact on our world and be remembered for it can be strong. We all want to know that we were significant to someone or something and that our passing through this world has meaning. This is why the search for meaning has existed as long as humans have and has been written about from antiquity to the present day. We all strive to make sense of why we're here and determine what we will leave behind when we're gone. Finding purpose, meaning, and significance—particularly when they're related to your aspirations and core values—provides intense and enduring drive over the course of your life. It's rocket fuel for your psyche and soul.

I spoke briefly about *empowerment, trust, and autonomy* earlier. These are aspects of drive that can be both internal and external, dependent upon circumstance. Although it can be argued that others must bestow trust, empowerment, and autonomy on you (which is true in certain situations), you can also manufacture them. These drivers are intangibles that you can wield to build and sustain yourself. To gain and sustain others' trust in you (as spouse, parent, sibling, son/daughter, community member, leader, coworker, role model) can be a powerful driver. It supports your senses of self-worth and significance, among other things. When others believe in you—in your sense of ethics, competence, judgment, and experience— this naturally feels good. It's life-affirming.

Autonomy and empowerment are related subjects, and both can motivate intrinsically. There's a fundamental need to maintain our position as captains of our own ships—to be the author of our life stories. The freedom and power we have to do so are drivers that have spawned countless revolutions and underpinned important cultural and civil rights movements. The needs for equality, fairness, and justice are entwined with the ability to determine our own fates and obtain the power to support that aim.

When you have the discretion to make decisions that impact your relationships, life, and career, these endeavors are more rewarding and meaningful. You're allowed to wield more of your knowledge, experience, and talents, which is why you possess those things in the first place. The Ferrari between your ears needs to be out on the road, where it's meant to be, not stuck in the garage under a cover all the time. Whether it's determining how to execute our job duties or deciding who to form and maintain relationships with, we all seek the ability to do so for ourselves and drive the direction our ships will travel in.

Challenge, progress, and achievement comprise another internal driver. You acquire knowledge, skills, and experience and hone your master talents. You want to use them, as these things are only valuable when they're exercised. Tasks that are menial and simple don't stretch your mental muscles enough to contribute to their growth—and do little to motivate you as a result. Challenges that appear as far too difficult and unlikely to result in achievement don't drive you forward either. It is challenges that test the bounds of your expertise and have some reasonable chance for success that will drive you most, particularly when they're aligned with your personal interests and purpose.

When you perform well on these challenges, it's often called operating in your *sweet spot*, which is "… the intersection of your motivations and your greatest strengths. When you are operating in your sweet spot, you feel inspired to do great things and confident that you can accomplish them because you are using your strengths. Having an awareness of what motivates you and understanding your strengths and weaknesses enables you to discover your sweet spot."[17]

The size of the challenge affects the feeling of accomplishment you gain from meeting it successfully. We all want to feel like we are 'good' at something and to experience the sweet taste of success. It affirms us and proves our worth to ourselves and others. Accomplishment boosts your self-esteem and sustains your drive to achieve even more. The momentum of winning is as powerful a motivator as a losing streak can be damaging to our sense of self-worth. The rapturous feeling of overcoming significant challenges in your life and achieving great things causes the brain to say, "More dopamine please." The way to maintain that pleasurable feeling is to find another mountain to summit.

As you undertake the challenges of your life that you've decided are meaningful for you (or that you have been volunteered to accomplish at work!), a sense of forward movement helps drive you further. The progress that you feel is evidence you're applying your talents and experience effectively, and this spurs you to work your way toward the next road marker.

This is why the act of setting goals and breaking significant challenges down into milestones is such a valuable part of performance management. It allows you to focus your efforts and provides a steady flow of motivational fuel that helps you eat the elephant, one bite at a time. Since overcoming challenges and accomplishing meaningful aims are also connected to your sense of purpose, meaning, and significance, achievement can be an extremely powerful driver.

Inclusion and affiliation are also primary internal needs that motivate our thoughts, feelings, and behaviors. Affiliation was recognized by Abraham Maslow, a pioneering twentieth-century psychologist, as forming part of the human hierarchy of needs that still bears his name today. It's been said that no man is an island, which means that human beings only thrive when they're connected to others. A sense of normalcy, feeling that we're good enough to be included in the group, access to support, and establishment of purpose and meaning can all be by-products of affiliation.

We know that loneliness and isolation can have significant negative effects on our physical and mental wellbeing. In some societies, isolation is even used as punishment (e.g., within the prison system), and no one likes being shunned from the groups to which they want to belong. Whether we say we are Freemasons, chartered accountants, teachers, lawyers, Christians, Hindus, Muslims; Ironman finishers, Olympians, conservatives, liberals, or any other group to which we choose to belong, there is normally pride and self-identity wrapped up in our participation. There are psychological benefits that wouldn't exist if you were alone. The motivation for inclusion is closely related to affiliation and satisfies the need to be a part of the narrative and decision-making process of matters that affect your life—both at home and at work. When you have advanced knowledge and a voice, you feel more valued and empowered and can take active measures to coauthor the story of your life.

The last primary internal motivator is *personal growth and learning*. You may view this as a part of personal progress—that your journey as a human being is to grow your knowledge, talent, and experience, particularly in ways that align closely with your core values.

Part of the human need for meaning is to make sense of the world, to understand tomorrow what you don't today and to explain how and why events happen. Seeking knowledge and growing your talents may also be seen as a personal challenge; a valued goal or aspiration to be worked toward. Master craftsman, PhD awards, graduating high school or university, and gaining professional designations may all signal that you've scaled some intellectual peak and have attained a level of knowledge valued by society. Those who prize learning and personal growth seek to continually be better versions of themselves. This can drive our behavior strongly at times. We spend significant amounts of time, effort, and money in our quest to gain knowledge and hone our talents when learning and growth are deeply valued.

So, we all have internal and external motivators that drive what we think, how we feel, and what we do. The types and mix of drivers are different for each of us, and identifying and using them is key for self-awareness and fulfillment. Neither internal or external motivators are 'good' or 'bad,' but it's important to understand their nature and that an overreliance on external motivators can leave us prone to the dangers of circumstance and others' whims.

- *What are the two internal motivators you identify most with?*
- *What are the three most important motivators (internal or external) for you?*
- *What motivators are most powerful for you during times of challenge and adversity?*

EXTERNAL SELF-AWARENESS

Tasha Eurich aptly stated, "… when we see our reflection in a mirror, it's easy to conclude that this is the only, and therefore the most accurate, representation of ourselves. It's far easier and safer to gaze at our reflection than face the possibility that others might not see us the same way. But gazing inward is a necessary but not a sufficient condition for true insight."[18]

While introspection is important to self-awareness, the way you see yourself is only one perspective. As others can generally provide you more objective viewpoints on yourself, gaining this external and less-filtered perspective is a valuable aspect of emotional intelligence, performance, and personal growth. If you're to see the whole portrait of yourself—not just the profile view—you've got to seek, understand, and use external feedback.

The process of seeking feedback is complex to our psyches but unbelievably simple in practice. The complexity comes from our inclination to place the value of our own view of ourselves above what others think. In a me-first world where we're encouraged to self-promote and constantly broadcast what we're thinking, feeling, and doing on social media, we seem predisposed to send information about ourselves out rather than taking it in. We're told not to allow others to rain on our parade and concentrate only on the positive in our lives. Couple this lack of interest in others' honest views of us with the reluctance to seek feedback because we fear it may be negative or conflict with our own perspective, and we have a recipe for continued self-ignorance. "We can't take or receive feedback if we are incapable or uninterested in hearing from outside sources. We can't recognize opportunities—or create them—if instead of seeing what is in front of us, we live inside our own fantasy. Without an *accurate* accounting of our own abilities compared to others, what we have is not confidence but delusion."[19]

The cure for this malady is, of course, to do the simplest thing: just *ask* for feedback. Others interact with you based on their thoughts and opinions of you. If you're to build and manage relationships successfully, manage conflict, gain credibility, wield influence, and engender trust, it's important to know how you're perceived by others.

There are plenty of people who, believing they know themselves well, plow their way through life's interactions, remaining blissfully ignorant of others' contempt for them. We've all known such people, or maybe been there ourselves at one point or another. It can be painful and embarrassing to witness.

If you ask for feedback from others in order to avoid this, make sure you're sincere. People can easily identify false requests or someone fishing for compliments from those they know have no interest in truly hearing the opinions of others. If you ask for the thoughts and opinions of others, be genuine in your request. In addition, when you receive feedback, remember not to become defensive about it. Remember, you asked for it, and some of the feedback is bound to be constructive. There's a temptation to devalue or dismiss negative feedback altogether, particularly if it directly contradicts your view of yourself. Resist that urge. The comments you receive about where you can improve are the most valuable, even though they may sting a bit. Feedback that is all wine and roses is of limited use and doesn't get to the real truth about how you're perceived.

The more you ask for—and demonstrate your sincerity in using—feedback for benign reasons, the greater the quantity and quality of it you will receive. There are other benefits to feedback as well. "When you regularly seek feedback, others become more inclined to tell you what they really think, thereby increasing your opportunities to learn. But there's another benefit—a hidden one—to asking others to share their opinions: people tend to think highly of those who consistently ask for critical feedback."[20] If you don't understand the feedback or need more detail, be sure to ask clarifying questions. Ensure others know the intent isn't to challenge their point of view but merely to understand it better.

I would also advise you to gain feedback from a variety of people. In the workplace, this is often termed 360-degree feedback as the process seeks the viewpoints of bosses, peers, subordinates, internal customers, and other coworkers in order to paint a holistic view of your behavior. Some organizations even have formal tools for gathering 360-degree feedback as part of annual appraisal and leadership development processes. Using the same technique outside of work is no less valuable for your self-awareness and personal growth. Remember that feedback is one person's viewpoint of you and your behavior; it's not *the* truth and has to be put in perspective of both your own and others' viewpoints. The credibility of feedback sources also needs to be taken into account.

Feedback can either be constructive or destructive in nature. Constructive feedback is specific, designed to help you, aimed at your behaviors, and respectfully given. Destructive feedback is the opposite. You need to take this into account as you analyze and assess the worth of feedback while remaining open-minded and resisting the temptation to be dismissive. Not every piece of feedback from every source is going to hold value for you. Try to find value where you can and if—after taking as objective and nonjudgmental a look as you can— you cannot find worth in it then move on.

Be sure to thank people for their feedback. It takes courage to provide it, particularly if it contains some constructive comments about where you can improve. People don't have to provide feedback to you at all, much less honest and useful feedback, so treat it with the appreciation it deserves.

You also need to ensure you don't waste feedback. Make use of it where you can in order to increase your self-awareness, personally grow, and gain a more objective perspective of yourself. Like any data-gathering exercise, it's useless if you don't act on the information. As Justin Bariso states in *EQ Applied*, "We might compare the feedback we receive to an unpolished diamond. To the untrained eye, a freshly mined gem may not look valuable, or even attractive. But after the long and complex process of sorting, cutting, and polishing, its true value becomes obvious. In a similar way, learning to extract the benefits of criticism can prove to be an invaluable skill."[21]

- *Do you regularly seek feedback on yourself or wait for it to come to you?*
- *What tools do you use to gather feedback on yourself today? How often do you use them?*
- *Do you become defensive and dismissive when you receive negative feedback, or are you open to hearing where you can improve?*
- *Do you take the time to analyze and reflect on feedback, figuring out how you can best use it to become more self-aware and grow personally?*
- *Who is best-placed outside of work to provide feedback on your behavior and how you are viewed by others? What about within work?*
- *What is the one piece of feedback from someone that has proven to be most valuable for improving yourself?*

As you explore your self-awareness and consider both your internal and external perspectives, you may wish to consider your blind spots and the use of tools like the Johari window to explore the relationship between your own knowledge of yourself and others' knowledge of you. The Johari window is a two-by-two grid with "Known to Self" and "Unknown to Self" on one axis and "Known to Others" and "Unknown to Others" on the other.

	Known to Self	Unknown to Self
Known to Others	OPEN	BLIND SPOT
Unknown to Others	HIDDEN	UNKNOWN

JOHARI WINDOW

The "Open" quadrant indicates complete self-awareness (something that both you and others know about you), while the "Hidden" quadrant indicates partial self-awareness (something you know about yourself that others do not). Likewise, the "Blind Spot" indicates partial self-awareness (something others know about you that you do not realize about yourself). Finally, the "Unknown" quadrant is just that—something about yourself that neither you nor others have uncovered. This can be a useful tool in analyzing traits, motivators, fears, strengths and talents, aspirations, biases, and core values. Use it to both better understand your current level of self-awareness and consider whether actions need to be taken to become more self-aware in the future. Take the time to try it and see what you discover about yourself.

MINDFULNESS AND SELF-AWARENESS

Related to, but different from, self-awareness, "Mindfulness means *deliberately paying attention*. Intentionally focusing. Nonjudgmentally observing life and living as it occurs around you. Being aware of your surroundings through all your senses. If you are not paying attention, you don't know whether you are missing out on something that matters to you!"[22] This isn't about being aware of yourself, or how others perceive you; it's about being fully engaged with your surroundings—being in the moment and sensitive to the environment around you.

Mindfulness is much more difficult than it sounds. Today's world bombards the senses and moves quickly. We can be contacted anywhere, anytime, in many ways. Ding! An email is received on our smartphone. We instinctively access it. Ding! A message notification arrives on WhatsApp. Ding! Another notification via text message comes in. Ding! And there's a notification from Facebook that someone liked our post. Ding! Facebook Messenger. Ding! Instagram. Ding! The seller on Ebay just changed the price of that motorcycle you've been wanting. Ding! Someone is reaching out on LinkedIn. Ding! News alert. Ding!

Our mind processes information one "Ding!" at a time, and our attention span can be about as long as Dory's memory in the children's movie *Finding Nemo*. The present rarely has our full attention. We may be standing somewhere, but our minds are either back an hour ago, worrying about one of those "Ding!" messages, or has already skipped ahead to an hour in the future, when the next work meeting starts, or the kids have to be picked up from school, or we have to leave for the dentist and are worried about traffic, or … , or …

You get the picture.

The inability to engage fully in the moment and provide it complete attention causes a number of negative consequences. The first is a continual state of anxiety. It may be low level and working in the background, or it might be more serious. If you're constantly skipping forward and backwards, replaying issues in your head over and over or ruminating over events that haven't yet occurred, you're manufacturing a steady flow of anxiety and dis-ease for yourself.

The irony is that often, because of a lack of attention to the present, you add one more (actual) problem to your plate as you fail to notice your surroundings, don't listen and observe properly, or miss participating fully in conversation. You underperform relative to your potential in whatever you were supposed to be engaged in. That is also likely to reflect negatively to those who noticed your lack of attention to the task at hand.

When you're in the moment and fully engaged with your surroundings, numerous benefits accrue. In *Emotional* Agility, Susan David commented on the relationship between mindfulness and competence, stating, "By helping us focus, mindfulness also increases competence. It improves memory, creativity and our mood, as well as relationships, health and longevity in general. By really paying attention to what's going on around us, rather than ignoring it or just going along with the programme, we can become more flexible and insightful."[23]

From meditation, breathing, and visualization exercises, note-taking, and other ways of documenting observation, to initiatives that develop active listening and observation skills, there are a number of ways to improve your ability to be purposefully attentive to the world around you. Like any skill or aspect of personal growth, your ability to be mindful will grow with training and practice. If you're to improve your focus, decision-making, listening and questioning, observation, information-gathering, and critical judgment skills— all of which impact your performance in life's endeavors—then learning to be mindful is critical.

* * *

- *Do you regularly find that you have daydreamed or been otherwise inattentive to events, conversations, and surroundings? Do you struggle to consciously focus and be attentive for more than a few minutes at a time?*
- *Do you have trouble recalling the details of where you were, what you were doing, or what was said when you think about how you spent your time over the last day or two?*
- *Do you regularly become distracted by your messages and alerts on your phone/computer and check them during meetings and conversations?*
- *Do you often multitask? Do you work on your computer or look at your smartphone while others are interacting with you?*
- *Do you use note-taking, breathing/meditation exercises, and active listening/questioning as tools to help your mindfulness?*

* * *

EGO'S ROLE IN SELF-AWARENESS

Our perception of self-worth and self-identity—which we know as ego—distinguishes us from others and, in this sense, is useful.

We all know from observation and personal experience that when our ego is threatened, strong reactions can cause us to lose emotional control and act counterproductive to maintaining healthy relationships. When our ego becomes inflated to a point that our sense of self-importance is also distorted, there's a tendency to be dismissive and disrespectful to others. The more valuable we see ourselves, the less worth we may perceive in others.

When ego grows unchecked, particularly in leaders, there's significant potential for followers to feel alienated, discontent, devalued, and underutilized. Complaints rise, people leave the group, and morale and productivity wane. The gap between internal and external self-awareness can absolutely come down to ego. Ego, therefore, is an important facet of both self-awareness and self-control.

It isn't a simple, easy process to keep ego in check, but it is a very necessary one. It isn't simple because the self-narrative regarding our importance, intelligence, appeal, uniqueness, or other special qualities feels so very good. It affirms us. It confirms our value to the world around us. And it's easy for us to rationalize that conceit, self-centeredness, and narcissism are merely strong self-esteem and confidence. We tell ourselves that others are just jealous and don't understand us; they are trying to tear us down. The narrative is one of the frustrated genius who has to blaze the trail alone because no one is capable of truly understanding the burdens that greatness bears.

Novartis CEO Daniel Vasella is quoted in Bill George's *Discover Your True North*, stating, " … for many of us the idea of being successful is intoxicating. It is a pattern of celebration leading to belief, leading to distortion. When you achieve good results, you are celebrated, and you begin to believe that the figure at the center of all that champagne toasting is yourself. You are idealized by the outside world, and there is a natural tendency to believe what is written is true."[24] When success doesn't organically flow in the usual fashion, we've never been more capable of manufacturing our desired realities to satisfy our need for significance and compete with the fantasy achievements of our social media connections. As Ryan Holiday puts it in *Ego is the Enemy*:

> Now more than ever, our culture fans the flames of ego. It's never been easier to talk, to puff ourselves up. We can brag about our goals to millions of our fans and followers—things only rock stars and cult leaders used to have. We can follow and interact with our idols on Twitter, we can read books and sites and watch TED talks, drink from a fire hose of inspiration and validation like never before (there's an app for that). We can name ourselves CEO of our exists-only-on-paper company. We can announce big news on social media and let the congratulations roll in. We can publish articles about ourselves in outlets that used to be sources of our objective journalism.[25]

The root of the problem with this story lies in the fact that we are unreliable sole narrators of our lives. We may be paper tigers. Pools that are broad but shallow. Form, and not substance.

There's a significant appeal in believing we are special and superior to those around us; we want to believe it, and we want others to believe it too. The potential for distortion from this is significant. It's always easier to look 'out there' for an explanation of why others don't understand or want to interact with us. It's not about our shortcomings; it's about theirs. The rose-colored lenses through which we view ourselves naturally lead us to conclude that the flaws and problems must lie elsewhere.

The irony is that when we confirm this to ourselves, we fail to seek the feedback necessary to keep ego in perspective, and it grows unchecked. If we think the problem isn't within us and we're already a successful expert, we don't need to seek counsel, engage in further learning, or solicit the input of others. A fragile ego causes us to fiercely defend it. It has an overriding need for self-preservation, and any encroachment or perceived insult to it causes a strong reaction. You've likely run into people who deliberately provoke conflict and say they are just marking their territory. That's an indication they have a wafer-thin ego. Remember, there's a distinct difference between confidence and a reasonable sense of your own worth and arrogance and disrespectfulness. The latter will not endear you to anyone, and it also won't sustain your position or your achievements. No one identifies narcissism as a positive quality.

So, what are the antidotes to egotism and disproportionate self-love?

The first is to regularly solicit external feedback. An increase in external self-awareness can counterbalance weak internal self-awareness and inflated ego by providing a regular flow of others' perspectives. When you understand that only you believe you can walk on water, you learn to keep your feet planted on firmer ground in future—which positively impacts others' perceptions of you.

Feedback is a valuable tool *if* it is sincerely reviewed and not dismissed. You learn what others think of you—their interpretation of your behaviors, strengths, weaknesses, performance, motivators, fears, and potential. There are no doubt gaps between yours and others' viewpoints to study and reconcile. Just remember that it's useless to argue that there is some objective truth out there that is different than the perceptions of others. Our perceptions *are* our realities. They drive our thought, emotion, and behavior.

It's a futile exercise to argue that the opinions others have of you are unfair or untrue. If you want to change others' perceptions of you, then you must change your own thoughts, feelings, and behaviors rather than trying to change their minds. Your thoughts, feelings, and behaviors are what fueled those perceptions in the first place—and you have the power to control them. Take the feedback and do something with it or it's wasted on you. Come up with a plan to use the feedback after you've analyzed it. Decide which aspects of yourself are most crucial to your personal growth and fulfillment and whether there are thoughts, emotional reactions, and behaviors that you can improve. Set goals and deadlines and solicit help and training from others where appropriate. Make sure to have follow-up scheduled so that you can hold yourself accountable for improvement.

Ego can be controlled, too, by remembering that none of your successes and accomplishments were yours alone. There's always someone or something that contributed and may have even been the primary reason for your achievement. Focusing on this helps you take the spotlight off of yourself and acknowledge others. Whether it involved the help of family, friends, mentors, teachers, bosses, coworkers, a kind stranger, or simply the benevolence of circumstance, you did not get to where you are today alone. Acknowledge the help, at least in your own mind (and hopefully to those who assisted you), and your humility will help put ego in check. There's always someone or something else to thank—at least in part.

If you think you're unable to do so, let me tell you about Jonas Salk, who was credited with discovering the polio vaccine. Salk failed to acknowledge the contributions of his lab assistants and others on the team, who made substantial contributions toward the discovery of the vaccine, during his Nobel Prize acceptance. The failure to credit his team was considered a horrible oversight by the scientific community, and he was shunned by it from that point on.

I also recommend finding a mentor or teacher. You have to take the first step in order to do so: admit that you aren't perfect and that others may know more than you, or be more talented than you, in certain areas you want to improve. Mentors humble us by demonstrating that we haven't reached their level of mastery yet. They can also help us discover how further improvement will benefit our personal growth journey. They're a third party who can help hold us accountable for using feedback and working on areas of focus.

Mentors also periodically hold a mirror up to us to help us remain grounded when we prematurely feel we've reached the summit of our expertise. The poet Ralph Waldo Emerson said, "In my walks, every man I meet is my superior in some way, and in that I learn from him." Seek out these people, realizing that no one knows everything about everything—not even you.

Analyzing your successes helps keep ego in check as well. In doing so we're likely to discover others to attribute our success to and ways we could have responded that might have been even more effective. It helps us understand cause and effect, and that surely uncovers causes beyond "because I'm brilliant!" These external causes remind us that the alignment of other people and things also contributes to success. There's a Chinese proverb that says, "Be like the bamboo. The higher you grow, the deeper you bow." Remain humble and honor those who support you along the journey. If you lift them up, they will do the same for you when they experience success—learning from your good example of humility.

Reflect, too, on how others respond to you. Do others generally avoid contact with you and you have to initiate interaction with them? Do you find people, when cornered into interacting with you, generally minimize the conversation and find reasons to quickly leave? If you're in a leadership role, do others rarely come to you with proactive updates on their progress? Do your phone calls go to voicemail most of the time? Are others defensive, offering excuses quickly for issues that occur? Do they rarely provide you feedback, and if asked for their opinion, always agree with you?

If you said yes to any of the questions above, those are signs you have relationship problems that may stem from ego. Don't dismiss these signs. They are telling you something indirectly. You need to periodically assess the quality and number of your relationships. If you find that, outside of necessary work contact, few people engage with you and have social conversations then that's a sign of fragile, transactional relationships. Take the time to consider whether your ego may play a part in inhibiting your relationships, whether within or outside of the workplace.

- *Do you almost always think you are the smartest one in the room? Do you regularly feel a sense of superiority over others?*
- *Are you prone to strong emotional reactions when your intelligence or decisions are questioned or feel that someone has encroached on your territory?*
- *Do you need to be 'right' all the time and win every argument or debate, even at the expense of relationships?*
- *Are you dismissive of constructive feedback? Do you find that others have either stopped providing you constructive feedback or any feedback altogether?*
- *Are your relationships superficial and largely confined to interactions that you and others need in order to accomplish work goals?*
- *Do you have a teacher or mentor? Do you continue to learn, or do you believe you have learned all that's necessary in order to function well in work and life?*

SELF-CONTROL: MANAGE YOUR THOUGHTS AND EMOTIONS

Having become aware of yourself, both from your own and others' perspectives—and having considered your ego's place in relationships—you've begun to lay the foundation for self-control. This is the next important facet of emotional intelligence. Self-control allows you to mold your realities in a way that serves yourself and others well. There's considerable evidence that our happiness and fulfillment in life doesn't rely on whether or not we experience challenges, setbacks, tragedy, or the cruel twists of fate; it instead depends on the views we take of those things and the responses we choose.

You have this power, no matter your circumstances, until you decide to let your mind take it away. Only you can tell yourself you're powerless, you're a victim, life is unfair, and your current state is a problem that will persist. No one can poison your psyche like you can. You can be your own worst enemy, which also means you can be your greatest savior. Just think of the awesome power in that! You can become your own superhero, but only if you allow your mind to reveal its secret identity to yourself and the world.

Ian Tuhovsky reminds us, "**Take responsibility for your own emotions, as you are the one causing them**. Every single emotion you experience is an effect of the thoughts you think every day. Depending on what beliefs you have about yourself and what images of your future you create, so you will feel. You will be a slave to other people's opinions and words, unless you decide to take action."[26]

If you can truly internalize accountability for your thoughts, feelings, and actions, you can unlock the positive potential in yourself. In doing so, you build the ability to become more resilient, respond more constructively to stress, react effectively to changes in your life, and grow the determination to see long and arduous tasks through. At least one of these ingredients is present in almost all tales of greatness, and you have the ability to build that story with yourself as the main character.

SELF-CONTROL MEANS *CHOICE*

As we have discussed, you have choices about how the happenings of your life are interpreted. Is something a challenge or opportunity? Failure or learning lesson? Death of one part of your life or a new beginning? Did you lose love or find yourself? Are you the passenger in your own life or the captain of your own ship? Even in events that most people would agree represent 'bad' circumstances or tragedy, you have the opportunity to choose how you interpret something, and in doing so, how you feel and act as a result of that viewpoint.

This isn't some naïve, Monty-Python-esque attempt to tell you to "always look on the bright side of life." It's perfectly natural to experience sadness, regret, depression, helplessness, anger, and jealousy, and you'll continue to experience them throughout your life. How you change your self-narrative about the circumstances that cause them, however, can lead you to experience negative or harmful emotions less often and with less intensity. That also allows you to hit pause and not act on negative emotions as often prior to changing the narrative to one that allows for a more constructive response. In *Learned Optimism*, Martin Seligman says:

Many things in life are beyond our control—our eye color, our race, the drought in the Midwest. But there is a vast, unclaimed territory of actions over which we can take control—or cede control to others or to fate. These actions involve the way we lead our lives, how we deal with other people, how we earn our living—all the aspects of existence in which we normally have some degree of choice. The way we think about this realm of life can actually diminish or enlarge the control we have over it. Our thoughts are not merely reactions to events; they change what ensues.[27]

Don't cede your power and control over the space between what provokes you and your response. Viktor Frankl asserted that very space allows you freedom, even in the direst of circumstances, to choose your thoughts, feelings, and actions rather than allow them to be instinctive, mindless *reactions* to circumstance. Allow them to become *proactions*— ones consciously chosen in alignment with your values. Create a more dispassionate view based on self-awareness and the intention to draw positive meaning from events. Detachment is a contributor to this and is a perspective that takes practice and intention to use.

Rather than immediately react to events based on your current filters of reality, try to view circumstances from the perspective of an outside observer. What would they think? What various ways could they rationally explain what has happened to you? What lessons or positives would they say can be drawn from the experience? What suggestions might they make for coping with it and overcoming obstacles? What advice do you believe they might give regarding how you should think and behave as a result of your circumstances?

Your vast power over events is because of the way you interpret of them. The way you think is the way you feel, and the way you feel determines your actions. You can choose to suffer or hope, to ruminate or learn, to grasp opportunity or wallow in crisis. American sports coach Lou Holtz summed it up nicely when he said, "Life is ten percent what happens to you and ninety percent how you respond to it." So, emotional control is about the choice you impose upon your interpretation of life and its events. You're not just responding to reality when you do so; you're actually manufacturing reality for yourself. And who wouldn't want a reality that is more positive, constructive, happy, hopeful, fulfilling, and grateful?

- *Do you use your ability to change your environment in order to change your thoughts and feelings about a situation?*
- *When events happen that cause you pain, suffering, or anger do you try to take the view of a detached observer in order to draw meaning from it and control your reactions?*
- *When others do something that causes you anger or hurt, do you try to understand why a rational person might act the way they did in order to better understand their actions?*
- *When you notice your instinct to react strongly to an event, do you create some space to allow yourself to gain perspective and control your emotions before responding?*

IDENTIFYING AND CHALLENGING ASSUMPTIONS

The basis of all interpretation is assumption. We infer the thoughts, feelings, intentions, and actions of others, as well as outcomes. We do this based on our past experiences, prior observations of others, and our values, core beliefs, and attitude. We filter these inputs through our minds and, based on our own unique lens of the world, we produce our reality. The problem with this is that our lens isn't clear, clean, and undistorted. As we've discussed, our assessment of our own knowledge, talents, abilities, and behaviors is likely to be skewed; it follows that our interpretation of the world around us is also likely to be the product of distorted assumption. As Martin Seligman puts it:

> We can more or less easily distance ourselves from the unfounded accusations of others. But we are much worse at distancing ourselves from the accusations that we launch—daily—at ourselves. After all, if *we* think them about ourselves, they must be true. Wrong! What we say to ourselves when we face a setback can be just as baseless as the ravings of a jealous rival … It is essential to stand back and suspend belief for a moment, to distance yourself from your pessimistic explanations at least long enough to verify their accuracy. Checking out the accuracy of our reflexive beliefs is what disputation is all about.[28]

Our instinctive, emotional reactions do not represent detached objectivity. This is especially true when it comes to assessing our interactions with others or the implications of the important circumstances of our lives. Our minds race to the end of the story, commonly through the window of worst-case scenario and catastrophe.

Alternatively, we infer others' intentions based on our own beliefs, values, and biases without much of an attempt to empathize with their thoughts and feelings. We label, stereotype, and dismiss: "He's overweight, so clearly he doesn't care about his health or appearance."; "She's an accountant, so she must be an introvert with few friends."; "She said she prefers to work on strategic, big-picture tasks so she must not be very detail-oriented."; "He said that maintaining relationships is most important in the workplace, so he wants to be everyone's friend rather than perform well."

Like you, I've witnessed (and made) assumptions about people based on flawed rationale—or no logic at all—in order to fit preconceptions of reality. It's the person whose manager dismisses their potential for promotion, not based on evidence of current performance or future potential, but because of a personality clash. Or it's the manager we decide is 'bad' or unfair because they hold us accountable for coming to work on time each day or deliver feedback we disagreed with. Or it's the partner we decide is incompatible with us because we don't see eye to eye on one specific issue.

We all can fall prey to searching for data and evidence to support our assumptions, rather than exploring whether the assumptions themselves may need rethinking. This reverse logic is a common way of ensuring our worldview remains intact and our egos unthreatened.

This twisting of logic to preserve our current sense of reality is also common to 'the Chimp'—our emotional selves that Steve Peters describes in his creative book *The Chimp Paradox*.[29] You can enhance your emotional control when you're overtly aware you are using assumptions to drive thought and feeling—and you identify and challenge those assumptions. Many assumptions you make may be based on incomplete information, flawed logic, and interpreting others' actions based on your own values and beliefs. Challenging whether these views are appropriate helps you decide whether to persist with your assumptions or consider changing them.

Even if an assumption is factually accurate or logical, it may not always be helpful. You have the opportunity to assess, too, whether a more benevolent view of the world might help you construct a more useful reality.

For example, there's plenty of evidence to logically conclude that people do unspeakable harm to each other and have evil in their hearts. There's also ample evidence to conclude that people are kindhearted creatures capable of great love and caring. Which viewpoint serves you better? Only you can decide that.

Take the time to identify your underlying assumptions when considering how to interpret the events of your life. As Greenberger and Padesky state in *Mind Over Mood*, "Even though underlying assumptions lie 'beneath the surface' they are easy to identify if you know where to look. Since underlying assumptions guide our behaviors and emotional reactions, we know they are active when we want to change a behavior but find it very difficult to do so, when we are avoiding something, and/or when we have strong emotional reactions."[30]

Look for the triggering behavior to help you identify and test assumptions. When you test them, use facts, evidence, and logic. What do you believe the risks *really* are if a bad outcome occurs? What are the *realistic* chances of this bad outcome occurring? Are you *actually* powerless to influence events toward a more positive outcome?

Let's jump back to the overweight person we referenced earlier. What evidence do you actually have that they don't care about their appearance or health, other than your assumption that their weight indicates this? What has this person actually said or done that indicates they don't care about their health or appearance? Are there people you know who are not overweight and in poor health or appearance? Are their others you know who may be overweight who appear to be in good health? And in reference to the person we assume is not detail-oriented, why did we assume this to be the case? Does a preference for strategic, big-picture work *actually* evidence a lack of detail orientation? What do this person's work products evidence? Quality? Thoroughness? An eye for detail? Or the opposite?

We commonly make snap judgments based on superficial information. We filter the world through our own biases to come up with unfounded conclusions. Sometimes we are 'right' (or lucky) and other times we come up with 'wrong' assumptions. So, test your assumptions and invite others to also do so. Having the courage to allow others to scrutinize your assumptions and validate or challenge them will help you lay a better foundation for your thoughts, feelings, and behavior. It also allows for the time to be spent in a way that will more effectively regulate your emotions. You're creating the space between thought and action I mentioned earlier.

- *Do you interpret events and make assumptions based on beliefs, without understanding whether these beliefs are based on fact and logic or are irrational?*
- *When you have an immediate or strong emotional reaction, or strong belief, do you try to search for facts and evidence that support your interpretation after the fact?*

- *When you have strong emotional reactions, avoid an issue, or want to change a behavior but find it hard to do so, do you try to identify and challenge your underlying assumptions?*
- *Do you invite others to analyze and test the validity of your assumptions, or do you feel threatened by the prospect of having others do so?*

YOUR ATTITUDE DETERMINES YOUR ALTITUDE

Your prevailing perspective on events and prediction of outcomes—what we might call attitude—is the result of your pattern of interpretation. Attitude produces feelings about our current circumstances and future. In a self-supporting, circular manner, your feelings can then produce further thoughts that align with them in order to sustain your emotion. This can be self-destructive when you experience negative emotion. When we're angry, sad, or feeling helpless, we're often drawn toward thoughts that support the prevailing mood and dismiss information that contradicts our current emotions.

This process was also discussed by Greenberger and Padesky in *Mind Over Mood* and explains why it's sometimes difficult to transition out of negative emotion when your thoughts are compelled to feed negative emotions rather than starve them of attention.[31] Using the example of anger, Daniel Goleman asserts, "The longer we ruminate about what has made us angry, the more 'good reasons' and self-justifications for being angry we can invent. Brooding fuels anger's flames."[32]

Another way you can become entrenched in unproductive thoughts and negative emotions is through the natural tendency for *comparison*. This is fueled by a society that urges you to look at yourself and your life critically, against some idealized model, or view life as a contest with those around you. Do you have the perfect figure? Could your muscles be bigger? Do you have a six-pack or is it more like a twelve-pack? Lips too thin? Too many wrinkles? Bags under your eyes? Balding? Don't like your nose? Breasts too small or large? Eyelashes too thin? Carrying too much weight?

There's an ever-increasing number of ways you're able to 'improve' your body, leading you to discover more and more of the ways your physiology has let you down. The twenty ways society allowed you to identify physical flaws fifty years ago has now become a hundred. You almost certainly compare yourself not only to an ideal but to others as well. You may feel pretty good about your progress in the gym until some Adonis or supermodel strolls by in the supermarket. Then the self-critiquing starts all over again.

The tendency for comparison goes beyond physical appearance. There's a thousand ways you can compare yourself to others, which lead you to enter the race to keep up with the Joneses. There are countless ways for you to make yourself feel insignificant and inferior to others if you go looking for even just a little while.

Is your house as big or as nice as the neighbor's or your best friend's? Is the car as prestigious as theirs? Are you as popular? Do you have as many important people at your parties? Are your vacations as luxurious? Are your jobs as well-paid and important? Are your kids in as many clubs and sports? Do you have as many friends on Facebook, connections on LinkedIn, or Twitter followers?

Another way in which you can mire yourself in unproductive thought and emotion is by holding to a *fixed mindset*. A fixed mindset is the 'nature' approach of the nature/nurture debate, and it asserts that we're largely born with the talents and traits we possess and that these remain largely as they are during the course of our lives. This can lead to a state of fragile egotism, where you're driven to repeatedly demonstrate to yourself and others that you possess intelligence, influence, competitiveness, ambition, and talent. This is done to prove your adequacy for its own sake if you believe these qualities won't change much over time. In the workplace, the fixed mindset approach sometimes misuses point-in-time assessments—IQ tests, assessments of working personality, leadership traits or skills—believing that the person seen today is the same we would have seen years ago and will see years from now.

When you succeed, particularly in competition, a fixed mindset tells you that you truly are *superior* to others in some way. This egotism can threaten the health of your relationships. And when you fail, the opposite occurs; a fixed mindset approach tells you that you were not good enough in some way, and that this will only change if external circumstances change as your human qualities are immovable. You're now helpless—at the mercy of fate. Failures risk lingering in your mind and offer a much greater threat to your identity and self-esteem. The subject is discussed in depth by Carol Dweck in *Mindset*, which is an excellent read on the dynamics of fixed and growth mindsets and their influences on us.[33]

So, how do you manage your attitude about circumstances? Consider using the *growth mindset* approach. Although a fixed mindset might be comforting to the ego when you're successful, it is counterproductive when you fail. We all know people who were the shy introvert, lacking confidence or social skills, who blossomed over time into a seemingly different person. A growth mindset provides you hope that you can become a better version of yourself with time and effort, improving upon your perceived weaknesses and evolving your talents and knowledge. I don't ascribe to the fixed mindset approach and believe that those with a sense of self-superiority are guarding their egos through an insistence on explaining life via nature and not nurture.

When you adopt a growth mindset there's an opportunity to learn from every setback, every failure, every adverse circumstance—either those you personally experience or those you witness. In doing so, you come to know that your potential is transient precisely because you can learn, develop, and grow. And if failure or problems occur, you learn from them in order to overcome them next time. Misfortune becomes a temporary problem for you; one with specific causes. You are empowered to draw from challenging experiences in order to meet them more effectively in future. Martin Seligman outlines this further in *Learned Optimism* and how a learning perspective helps counter the fixed mindset that finds permanent and universal causes for misfortune that he describes as " … the practice of despair."[34]

The benefits of a growth mindset are also described by Susan David in *Emotional Agility*, who states, "The ancient Greek master of paradox, Heraclitus, said that you can never step into the same river twice, meaning that the world is constantly changing and thus always presenting us with new opportunities and situations ... The freshest and most interesting solutions often come when we embrace 'the beginner's mind,' approaching novel experiences with fresh eyes. This is a cornerstone of emotional agility."[35] A growth mindset doesn't obsess with judgment, determining whether circumstances are 'good' or 'bad.' The focus is instead on what you can learn and apply constructively in future from the experience.

When you adopt a learning perspective, you aren't enslaved by ego and the need to continually demonstrate your worth to yourself and others. You know you sometimes fail and face difficulties you don't always overcome well. But that isn't threatening because you can always rely on gaining wisdom and increasing the chances of success in similar future situations.

knowledge + reflection = wisdom

You are *not* your failures. A failure is a happening; an event. It ends, and so do its consequences. With a growth mindset you even get to choose, at least to some extent, whether the consequences are personally useful or not.

If failures and adversity do not threaten our sense of identity and self-worth, we expose ourselves to situations with greater risk and reward potential. We get creative; we innovate. One leader I worked with said he got to become an executive "by making more mistakes than most anyone else." I think what he *really* meant was that he got to make more mistakes than anyone else, *and* he learned from them to fuel even greater achievements.

The by-product of a growth mindset is the desire for unvarnished feedback. As Carol Dweck explains in *Mindset*, "If, like those with the growth mindset, you believe you can develop yourself, then you're open to accurate information about your current abilities, even if it's unflattering. What's more, if you're oriented toward learning, as they are, you *need* accurate information about your current abilities in order to learn effectively."[36]

Another tool that helps regulate attitude is *self-acceptance*. It's difficult in a world where we focus on idealized models of humanity, continual improvement, and lean processes to accept that we are 'good' enough at some point and practice self-compassion. The prevailing philosophy seems to be that once we do so, we're somehow inhibiting our personal growth and giving in to mediocrity and compromise.

Self-acceptance is *not* in conflict with a growth mindset; they're not mutually exclusive concepts. At what point can you decide to love yourself and still acknowledge your potential to grow personally and professionally? The answer is: at any point! But you have to *choose* to do so. This sounds naïve, but it's true. You *can* decide, at any point, that while you're not perfect, you are brilliant nevertheless—perhaps not in spite of your flaws, but because of them. Giving yourself a break does not mean giving up. Susan David says, "There's a misconception that you need to be tough on yourself to maintain your edge. But people who are more accepting of their own failures may actually be *more* motivated to improve. Self-compassionate people aim just as high as self-critical people do. The difference is that self-compassionate people don't fall apart when, as sometimes happens, they don't meet their goals."[37]

Reframing is common technique used to manage perspective on events and can help maintain emotional control. While this may be linked, directly or indirectly, to a growth mindset reframing invites us to take an alternative view of a situation—replacing our negative judgments with something more useful. This could be what we have learned from our circumstances, but is more commonly what is positive or interesting/novel about what happened. By doing so, and even listing the positive, interesting, and negative aspects of an event, we provide ourselves more choice about the perspectives we can take.

Price Pritchett, in *Hard Optimism*, states that "... reframing counters our tendency to overestimate problems and underestimate our ability to handle them successfully. It helps us regain emotional balance and see new possibilities we haven't considered before. Simply put, positive reappraisal creates space for optimism. It nurtures hope. It adds to your resilience. And it leaves you much less vulnerable to the harsh realities of the moment."[38]

We are able to literally create a new reality by telling ourselves: "I can choose to view this event as positive for the following reasons and interesting because of these few reasons. It's up to me." Reframing isn't quick or easy, and takes practice. The next time something happens in your life that you are inclined to view as 'bad,' ask yourself: "Why could someone else view this event as positive? Why would someone view this event as novel or interesting?" Taking the time to ask and answer these questions also allows you to re-establish perspective that got lost in initial, strong emotional reactions.

Gratitude is another resource for regulating your interpretation of events and the thoughts and emotions that result from them. We have a natural human inclination to seek *more*: more love, more attention, more respect, more knowledge, more power, more money, more material wealth. In doing so, we often compare ourselves to others—or to an ideal. This causes us discontent and amplifies the gap between what we have today and what we believe life should afford us.

At one point your parents probably said—annoyingly at the time—to be grateful for what you have already. There's something to this advice our parents gave. At its core, gratitude isn't about compromising, giving up on our dreams, or settling for mediocrity. It's about turning our hearts and minds away from discontent and toward positive emotions that serve us better. Our parents likely gained wisdom through hard experience—chasing more until the pursuit itself either had a negative impact on other aspects of their lives, or they obtained what they were after and realized that there's a point at which *more* is no longer fulfilling.

In *Hard Optimism*, Price Pritchett says, "Managing your outlook toward appreciation and thankfulness feeds the soul. It brings calm and contentment. It lifts your levels of happiness and hope. Gratitude will amplify your positive recollections about times past, and that in turn sets the stage for optimism about the future."[39] A mind that's calm, contented, and appreciative is likely in a much better place to see current and future opportunity—and exploit our current talents and experience for positive outcomes.

There are those who contend that poverty is a great motivator—that an overwhelming lack of contentment with our current circumstances fuels us to change them. But this transition can take place either from a negative perspective (i.e., I'm not happy with what I have and things must change) or a place of gratitude (i.e., I'm thankful for the people, experiences, and things that life has afforded me so far and am aiming to grow myself further in this direction.). The latter is a glass-half-full perspective that is far more useful.

It's been said that you can catch more bees using honey than you can with vinegar. If our aim is to have our minds catch more constructive, positive thoughts and transition them to useful emotion, it's very hard to do that starting from a place of discontent and negativity. Don't let adversity teach you to appreciate what you had after it's gone. Instead, be grateful for it while it's still around.

- *Do you ruminate over adversity and the circumstances of your life, or can you move on emotionally from difficulties?*
- *Do you allow problems and failure in one aspect of your life to negatively affect all the other areas of your life, or can you compartmentalize?*
- *Do you get carried away by gut reactions, or do you allow yourself and others to challenge the assumptions that lead you to negative thoughts and emotions?*
- *Do you continually compare yourself and your circumstances to others, concluding that you're inferior or missing out somehow, or do you practice self-acceptance?*
- *Are you rarely content and always seeking more, or do you reflect positively on your circumstances in order to practice gratitude?*
- *Do you reframe tough circumstances, failure, and adversity to find the knowledge and positivity you can glean from them?*
- *Do you demonstrate a fixed mindset, believing that people can do little to change themselves or impact their circumstances? Or do you*

believe that people can learn and grow in order to influence positive outcomes in their lives?

THE ROLE OF OPTIMISM

There can be profound differences between the impact positive and negative mindsets have on your interpretation of the world, just as with fixed and growth mindsets. We often quip that people are glass-half-empty or glass-half-full people—that some look for the silver lining in every cloud while others look for the cloud in every silver lining. This might be jokingly said, but the impact of the mindset you choose can be significant on your thoughts, feelings, actions, and outcomes. Your mindset can also affect your physical and mental health. A pessimistic mindset can make you dismiss options for problem resolution, generate feelings of helplessness and despair, and cause you to be mired in inaction.

Martin Seligman, in *Learned Optimism,* states that there's plenty of evidence to suggest that pessimists both give up more easily and become depressed more frequently. He also referenced experiments that showed a prevailing mindset of optimism or pessimism also affects academic and work performance, as well as physical health (and perhaps even longevity).[40]

With so much riding on your mindset choice, it's important to consider how optimism can benefit your emotional intelligence and fulfillment. Thibaut Meurisse, in *Master Your Emotions,* also discusses the importance of the optimism/pessimism choice. He asserts that our brain is an organ whose function is not to make us happy but to help ensure our survival. If that's true, happiness is not something we can just count on being delivered to us; it's something we have to generate by choosing the language we use to interpret events. It can be one of positivity, or one of negativity. If happiness isn't a natural state automatically generated by the brain, it takes effort on our part. We have to be the main player in the happiness manufacturing process. To prove his point, Meurisse references a study on that very subject:

Let me share an interesting study that will likely change the way you see happiness. This study, which was conducted in 1978 on lottery winners and paraplegics, was incredibly eye-opening for me. The investigation evaluated how winning the lottery or becoming a paraplegic influence happiness. The study found that one year after the event, both groups were just as happy as they were beforehand ... The influence of external factors is probably way less than you thought. The bottom line is this: Your attitude towards life influences your happiness, not what happens to you.[41]

While the study is quite dated now, it supports the argument that we are our only source of renewable energy for happiness. Events can drain or boost our energy supply based on how we interpret them, but in the end, only we can power ourselves emotionally. Eventually, we settle back into a state of emotional equilibrium despite triumph or tragedy as we adjust to our new normal—and that is influenced by optimism or pessimism.

Optimism tends to view 'bad' events or adversity as temporary and specific challenges to be overcome. Optimistic people perceive that there will be a return to a prevailing state of contentment before long. On the other hand, pessimists believe that life is a battle where adversity, problems, and struggle are the norm, occasionally broken up by short-term states of contentment.

When your body and mind are continually on alert, viewing threat as a constant that could come from anywhere, the drain on your emotional energy is significant and the negative physical and mental effects can add up. Pessimism and negativity are exhausting. Even the most finely tuned athlete eventually experiences injury when asked to run a marathon day after day.

Optimism, on the other hand, is like the experienced athletic coach who understands how to push us further and faster—over time and at the right times—to achieve victory. If you've ever observed world-class cyclists racing, you know riders in the peloton draft each other, conserving energy until the moment they make their winning move. No rider wins a Tour de France riding alone the entire race, up the mountains and against the winds. Optimism allows us to draft when times are tough so we can apply our talents when and where they matter most.

Daniel Goleman, in *Emotional Intelligence*, references research that found people who are hopeful "… share certain traits, among them being able to motivate themselves, feeling resourceful enough to find ways to accomplish their objectives, reassuring themselves when in a tight spot that things will get better, being flexible enough to find different ways to get to their goals or to switch goals if one becomes impossible, and having the sense to break down a formidable task into smaller, manageable pieces."[42]

Optimism, then, doesn't just brighten your mood for its own sake; it actually gives you additional resources to achieve your aims and become more fulfilled. The openness to consider alternative solutions rather than the closed-mindedness of pessimism (i.e., "No, that won't work. That won't work either.") gives you more ways to overcome adversity. Optimism also keeps you moving forward in the face of setbacks and failure. It reassures you that success is the natural result of additional effort and different remedies applied to the task at hand. Because failure and adversity are temporary and specific to the optimist, it's just a matter of being flexible enough to experiment and find the right solution applied in the right way.

So, having discussed the virtue of optimism as a means of emotional control and resource for self-fulfillment, how do you capture optimism in your life?

The first step is to acknowledge that, although you cannot always control your initial feelings in every situation, you can decide the general perspective through which you'll interpret them. You can make a conscious decision to use optimism as your filter, drawing the positive from the events in your life.

This might sound idealistic, but we've already established that you control your thoughts and that your feelings and actions derive from those thoughts. Likewise, the mindset that produces patterns of thought can be chosen. By holding yourself accountable for optimism, you go searching for light rather than clamoring toward the dark places in your mind. Using a prevailing attitude of optimism is a choice and applying it—particularly when you find yourself stumbling toward bleak thoughts—is also a choice.

One resource you can use to support optimism is positive affirmation. Self-talk that reminds you of your positive qualities, past successes, adversities conquered, and future potential helps increase your optimism regarding current and future circumstances. Self-talk involving the positive aspects of 'bad' events or circumstances also allows you to learn from them and take heart.

At a minimum, through optimism, you gain something from every happening in your life: knowledge and experience. When you make a habit of looking for the good in yourself and your circumstances, it's surprising how much you can find.

Martin Seligman, in *Learned Optimism*, discusses the techniques of *distraction* and *dispute* as tools to counter pessimism and build a positive outlook.[43] The first technique, distraction, is simply making a conscious effort to think of something else when pessimism strikes. This could include using an activity to take your mind off the problem. For instance, a hobby, exercise, or social conversation could be a distraction. The second technique, dispute, is fundamentally the same as challenging your assumptions. By either challenging the logic behind your pessimistic beliefs, or simply arguing for why a more positive approach would serve you better, you can overcome negative thoughts and beliefs.

Remember that you have the ability to influence your environment, and in doing so, you change the conditions that might otherwise have resulted in negativity. We have all been around pessimistic people in our lives and know they can infect our own thoughts with negativity. By avoiding pessimists and resisting the urge to commiserate with them when we do have to interact, we lessen our chances of slipping into a negative mindset.

We also know that, in contrast, seeking out positive and enthusiastic people increases the likelihood that optimism rubs off on us. Jeff Keller aptly reminds us of the effect of our mindset on others, stating, "… if given the choice, I'd rather be around people who are positive and full of life … as opposed to those who are negative and listless. It's like the old saying that everybody lights up a room—*some when they walk into the room … and some when they walk out!*"[44]

- *Do you make a conscious commitment to look for positivity in each event of your life, or do you easily fall into pessimism without thinking?*
- *Do you use positive self-talk to help boost your optimism, confidence, and self-esteem, or do you get stuck in negative conversations with yourself?*
- *Do you make a habit of interacting and commiserating with pessimists, or do you seek out a more optimistic crowd?*
- *Do you light up the room when you enter, or when you leave?*

AUTHENTICITY

A facet that contains elements of both character and emotional intelligence, *authenticity* is important for building trust with others—as well as for your personal fulfillment and happiness. One of the great ironies in life is that we spend our youth trying to fit in and our adulthood attempting to stand out. To support both efforts, you can find yourself putting on masks and trying to be someone other than who you really are. You might compromise your beliefs or values, failing to speak up in support of them at crucial moments. You may alter your appearance, manner, interests, and communication style in an effort to become another person. You may bow to peer pressure to say or do things that aren't aligned with your true self.

Sometimes these efforts are an attempt to mimic our respected role models, and other times they are designed for escaping what we see as a less-than-adequate self. At some point in our lives, we've all mixed up learning from others' positive qualities and adopting them to become better versions of ourselves with a directive to escape ourselves altogether. There's a massive difference between the two, and the internal conflict that stems from self-rejection and mimicry can eat away at our confidence and self-esteem. Soon, we convince ourselves that we are altogether not enough, and we lose our real identities in the shuffle of masks we wear.

Ryan Holiday, in *Ego is the Enemy*, reminds us of the fragile state of our lives when we judge ourselves constantly through the eyes of others, saying, " … each one of us has a unique potential and purpose; that means we're the only ones who can evaluate and set the terms of our lives. Far too often, we look at other people and make their approval the standard we feel compelled to meet, and as a result, squander our very potential and purpose."[45] The approval of others might feel good, but it can also be hollow and fleeting. Others may approve of you because you've agreed to walk *their* path, meet *their* standards, and play in *their* game. When these things align with your own values and belief system, it may feel genuinely good. When you've compromised your values, beliefs, morals, and priorities in order to gain that approval, the taste is bittersweet at best. Acceptance and achievement won inauthentically is like fool's gold; it might look pleasing to the eye, but it's not real.

While your intentions might be benign—to fit in with the crowd or win the approval and recognition of others—sacrificing your commitment to your values and beliefs is a high price to pay. It forces you to live in a state of perpetual self-conflict and dis-ease, knowing that you're not exhibiting your true self to the world. Eventually, your mask slips. Others see the disconnect between what you may say or do and how you really feel, and this tension inevitably causes a break between your shadow self and your true self. When others see it, your respect and place in the group is jeopardized. You've deceived yourself and others. While we all adapt our message and behavior to our audience, inauthenticity takes this too far—and is exhausting.

Authenticity is liberating. It releases you from feeling like the real you isn't 'good' enough to truly claim your achievements, even when you win approval or a place in a group. You no longer have to keep up multiple lives. When you finally release yourself from this burden, you understand that authenticity allows you to succeed or fail on your own terms, not as a manufactured shadow of yourself. In *EQ Applied*, Justin Bariso says:

Authentic people share their true thoughts and feelings with others. They know not everyone will agree with them, and they realize this is okay. They also understand that they aren't perfect, but they're willing to show these imperfections because they know that everyone else has them, too. By accepting others for who they are, authentic individuals prove relatable ... Authenticity doesn't mean sharing everything about yourself, with everyone, all of the time. It *does* mean saying what you mean, meaning what you say, and sticking to your values and principles above all else.[46]

Authenticity is almost impossible without self-acceptance. Free of the restraints that come with constantly measuring ourselves through the eyes of others, authentic people understand that they're the only people who live with themselves all day, every day. Having to live with ourselves, we must prioritize our own approval and contentment. Others' acceptance and recognition feels far better when won genuinely. If those things don't arrive our lives don't crumble, because we can still live content with who we really are.

We all have flaws and weaknesses. Living authentically doesn't mean accepting mediocrity or excusing poor behavior and performance. It means that we have the self-compassion to acknowledge that we'll stumble at times. While we work to improve, we know that perfecting ourselves is impossible. Humanity's very nature defies perfection. Authenticity also means we understand that those who try to crucify us for a lack of perfection are hypocritical. The occasional extreme behavior that comes from others when we stumble, particularly on life's inconsequential tasks, says far more about their ego and inauthenticity than it does our imperfections.

So, set down the burden of working to please everyone else as much as possible. That's a fool's game. As Thibault Meurisse, in *Master Your Emotions*, says, " ... don't make it your personal mission to change people's image of you. People are entitled to their beliefs and values, and they have the right to dislike you. They are free to interpret your actions and behaviors through their own filter. Part of your personal growth is to accept you don't have to be liked by everybody, and finally, you can be yourself."[47] You have to look in the mirror and be content with your own reflection—not use someone else's in order to judge yourself.

- *Do you regularly catch yourself acting out a character who is not reflective of your values, principles, and beliefs?*
- *Do you find yourself prioritizing the approval of others, or achieving some goal, above maintaining your belief system?*
- *Do you often feel that being your true self won't be enough for others around you?*
- *Do you fear expressing opinions and beliefs that may run counter to the majority or to the important people in your life?*
- *Are you content to talk about your flaws, mistakes, and weaknesses with others, or do you do your best to keep them hidden?*

Section Three
RESILIENCE AND STRESS MANAGEMENT

L ife provides moments of rapture, joy, triumph, pure love, hope, and true contentment. It also contains tragedy, sorrow, adversity, obstacles, and hostility. In fact, the latter remind us how sweet the former taste. We're unlikely to ever really understand the 'good' moments in our lives without knowing their opposite. Tragedy and triumph calibrate our experiences. They provide richness and depth that the middle ground of mild contentment cannot. We avoid apathy, even at the price of pain, because any feeling reminds us we're alive—and that is better than the alternative.

Today's societies perpetuate the myth of perfection as the norm. We have access to this myth twenty-four hours a day, every day. Every time we glance at our smartphone, turn on the television, or listen to the radio (you remember the radio, don't you?), we see and hear beautiful people doing impossible things and achieving spectacular outcomes. The message we receive is that extraordinary is the new ordinary, and ordinary, well, just isn't acceptable to the world at large anymore. As Elizabeth Day states in *Failosophy*, " … we live in an age of curated perfection, where social media encourages us to believe we are all celebrities in our own lives."[48] There's a quick and easy route to greatness, apparently, and a better version of you is only a couple of clicks and one credit card payment away.

The unfortunate message stemming from this perfection myth is that we can skip the hard work, effort, setbacks, and adversity that often accompany personal growth and achievement and just fast-forward to success. We have become entitled. Society *owes* us our piece of the good life, and if we can skip the hard lessons and trials, then of course we'd prefer to fast-forward our way there.

There's a show-me-the-money mentality in which we seek life's rewards before we pay our dues and truly earn them, and that has redefined—really, lowered—the standard of hard work. It's also led to the erosion of coping skills when life places obstacles in our path that we can't quickly and easily overcome. As Mark McGuiness states in his wonderful read *Resilience*, " ... the immature and unready want to have the good things without facing up to the fear. They want to order success like a pizza, or download it like a movie—instantly and easily. But success isn't like that."[49]

Adversity and trials are part of reality. You can't willingly accept the good times without understanding that you'll also be tested with problems and setbacks on your journey. Happiness isn't an end destination; it's found scattered along the path if you're willing to step over or around the occasional obstacles to find it.

Successfully overcoming life's challenges is an ability grown through practice. No pain, no gain, as they say. It's like lifting weights or training for a marathon. Each time you do so, you push yourself to go further, go faster, and carry a heavier burden. You go to an extent that wasn't possible for you before—until it was. The body breaks itself down to become stronger in the future. The hardcore fitness enthusiasts will tell you that pain is weakness leaving the body. My take is that pain signals your body and soul are growing stronger, but only when you face and overcome the pain sitting between you and the next step in your life's journey. Think repair, not despair. In *Attitude is Everything*, Jeff Keller says:

> *Adversity brings out our hidden potential.* After surviving a difficult ordeal or overcoming an obstacle, you emerge emotionally stronger. Life has tested you and you were equal to the task. Then, when the next hurdle appears, you're better equipped to handle it. Problems and challenges

bring out the best within us—we discover abilities we never knew we possessed. Many of us would never have discovered these talents if life hadn't made us travel over some bumpy ground. Adversity reveals to you your own strengths and capacities, and beckons you to develop those qualities even further.[50]

We've broadly introduced the concept of *resilience,* which is related to your ability to adapt, persevere, and overcome in the face of setbacks, obstacles, and adversity. Skills for remaining happy and successfully finding your way to the next step in your life journey—despite the problems you encounter—are crucial and can be learned. Like any other competency, you can grow it so that heart, mind, and body are better equipped for the challenges you face.

The concept of *stress* is also related to resilience. Stress is the body's reaction to perceived threats and results in both physical and mental responses to combat the perils we envision. There's a level of stress that can be useful, motivating you to rise to the challenge or—at its most basic level—survive. It's the fight or flight mechanism you use to protect yourself from harm. Like too much of anything, however, it can be bad for you.

We've all been in situations of extreme stress at some point in our lives and seen firsthand the problems it can create. Emotional difficulties, such as withdrawal, breakdown, depression, irritability, lashing out, and anxiety can occur. Our judgment can be clouded and decision-making negatively affected. Physical effects can be real too, and the relationship between stress and heart disease, heart attacks, sleep problems, asthma, diabetes, immunosuppression, and physically harmful coping habits (e.g., alcoholism, drug abuse, self-harm) has been studied. Building resilience and coping effectively with stress are two sides of the same coin, and in many cases, techniques for addressing one can have a positive impact on the other.

PROBLEMS AND POSSIBILITIES

Things are going great. The stars have aligned, and you're effortlessly coasting through each day. You have conquered life. Success and happiness appear to be available on tap for you. Until … a close relationship ends; you are blindsided by health problems; a personal tragedy occurs; you have an unexpected job loss; a friend or loved one passes away; or the world experiences a health pandemic. There are countless ways your success and happiness locomotive can derail. It can—and will—happen to you. It has almost certainly happened already at some point in your life. Falling down isn't hard; everyone does it from time to time. The question is whether you choose to get back up and put your train back on the tracks.

Like death, taxes, and change, adversity is an inevitable part of living. It's something we all experience periodically. Sometimes that adversity is on a small scale, and other times it seems enormous and insurmountable. However, there are possibilities in every problem—discoveries that overcome our hardship, a new perspective on our strengths and potential, or a blossoming of talent. After all, some of the most beautiful flowers grow in poor soil and harsh conditions. In *Success Through a Positive Mental Attitude*, W. Clement Stone aptly says, "*Every adversity has the seed of greater benefit.* Sometimes the things that seem to be adversities turn out to be *opportunities in disguise.*"[51]

Like many things, overcoming adversity is a practiced skill. Adversity can reveal opportunity if you're willing to be open to the valuable lessons and new possibilities accompanying hardship. That is your choice. You can decide to dwell in the land of regret and despair, wallowing in self-pity and failing to see the silver linings. You can be someone who looks for a problem for every solution. Or you can instead point your chin into the wind and look for solutions and meaning that inevitably accompany adversity. I don't believe that life's trials come without reason or meaning, and neither should you. You're stronger than that.

Peter Crone, "The Mind Architect," regularly references the fact that we are where we are, which is exactly where we're supposed to be right at this moment in time. He says something like, "What happened happened, and couldn't have happened any other way."

Now this might sound fatalistic, and the skeptic would point out that there's an endless stream of alternatives that could have led us away from where we stand at this moment in time. But in doing so, they'd miss the whole point: arguing with ourselves about what might have been is a futile effort because we don't possess the ability to travel back in time.

There's a difference between reflecting on what led you here, drawing meaning from it, and constantly ruminating about your problems. In the former instance, you only briefly visit the past for the purpose of gaining wisdom. The latter instance makes you a permanent resident of the past, unable to learn from it and to cope in the present. Elizabeth Day wrote a great read called *Failosophy*. In it, she says, "Being at peace with failure means I have very few regrets. Each time something has gone wrong, it has led me to where I am meant to be, which is right here, right now … the universe is unfolding exactly as is intended and that although we, as imperfect humans, can't hope to understand it all the time, life will generally teach us the lessons we need to learn if we are open to the possibility."[52] As sweet as success tastes, adversity and failure often teach us much more valuable lessons that lead us toward future fulfillment. Yes, those lessons come at a price, but nothing worth having ever comes easy.

- *Do you believe that adverse situations provide you opportunity or only problems?*
- *Do you reflect on the purpose and meaning you can gain from adversity, or instead just ruminate about the difficulties it causes you?*
- *Are you comfortable with the idea that both successes and failures have brought you exactly where you need to be, right here, right now?*

PERCEPTION IS REALITY

You are the author of your life. You create and tell the story—both to yourself and others. Whether you write a tragedy or a dramatic tale of triumph and happiness is up to you. Everyone starts with a blank sheet of paper and the power of choice, and each of us then crafts our own unique tale.

Our perspective colors the story significantly; it's the hidden hand that writes for us. No two people perceive an event in exactly the same way, based on the same values, principles, and past experiences. What is desirable or 'good' to one person is 'bad' and something to be avoided to another. We also know that an event viewed at one point in our own lives might be seen as undesirable and at another point be seen as fortunate.

During challenging times we can lose perspective, allowing our thoughts to wander down dark corridors in our minds and take up residence there. We become mired in despair, telling ourselves a tragic story starring us as the victim, powerless against dark forces and unfortunate events. Before long, we've deceived ourselves into helplessness and hopelessness because we've told the lie enough times to convince ourselves it's the truth. While there are undoubtedly unfortunate circumstances and adversity that everyone encounters in their lives, whether something is an enduring tragedy that's impossible to overcome depends on the story we craft. In *QBQ! The Question Behind the Question*, John Miller says:

> Yes, bad things happen: The economy sours, our business struggles, the stock market tumbles, jobs are lost, the people around us don't follow through, deadlines are missed, projects fail, good people leave. Life is full of these. But still, stress is a choice, because whatever the "trigger event," we always choose our own response. We choose to react angrily. We choose to stuff our emotions and keep quiet. We choose to worry … Different people have different reactions to the same situation. Stress is a choice. Stress is also the *result* of our choices. When we choose to ask a question like "Why is this happening to me?" we feel as if we have no control. This leads us to a victim mindset, which is extremely stressful.[53]

Just as each person views the world and its happenings differently, we know we also have the ability to alter our interpretation of events and our surroundings. We own our thoughts. We have the freedom to choose them, which means we are also accountable for the thought choices we make. We've discussed challenging our thoughts as part of emotional intelligence, and the process is no different here.

The ability to identify and challenge seemingly irrational thoughts is an important part of resilience. When you catch yourself thinking crazy thoughts about a situation, you have to call yourself on it. When you tell yourself that life isn't fair, that you are repeatedly victimized by others or bad luck, that you are uniquely flawed and destined to fail, are powerless to act, and simply not as 'good' as others, you must challenge those useless perceptions. They serve no purpose. Challenge the assumptions behind those thoughts.

Why would a rational person think this way? What *real* evidence do I have to support this conclusion? What are the *real* chances of this conclusion happening? If I relayed these thoughts to my most trusted friend, how would they respond?

Remember, if you're in an intense emotional state, you will look for evidence to support your crazy thoughts. You've got to be able to step out of your head long enough to play the part of a detached observer, bringing perspective back to your current situation. It keeps you from pole vaulting over mouse droppings in your mind. When you pole vault over mouse droppings, you use precious emotional energy that's better conserved to cope with the real challenge at hand.

In addition to challenging irrational thoughts, *reframing* is another useful technique that can help you build resilience and improve your ability to cope with stress and adversity. Reframing helps put the situation you're facing in a more useful perspective so that you can cope with and overcome problems more effectively.

For instance, when a situation occurs that seems 'bad,' remember that 'bad' is only a label that you have instinctively attached to it. Are there any reasons someone else might interpret the situation as 'good'? What useful lessons can you take from experiencing the situation? What opportunities might arise as a result of your circumstances? When you look at this circumstance a month or a year down the road, how big will the problem look in the rearview mirror as you continue to travel away from it? Reframing requires you to step out of your mind in order to effectively ask and answer these questions, which is why self-awareness is such an important aspect of emotional intelligence.

The goal of both reframing and challenging irrational thoughts is to gain a more constructive perception of your circumstances. In doing so, you improve your ability to manage your stress and cope with the adversity that will periodically come your way. As Ryan Holiday explains in *The Obstacle is the Way*, "It takes skill and discipline to bat away the pests of bad perceptions, to separate reliable signals from deceptive ones, to filter out prejudice, expectation, and fear. But it's worth it, for what's left is *truth* ... We will see things simply and straightforwardly, as they truly are—neither good nor bad. This will be an incredible advantage for us in the fight against obstacles."[54]

If we're busy fighting the imaginary demons that stand between us and conquering adversity, little is left to deal with real problems. When we erase judgment from circumstance, we also remove many of the obstacles to resolving our situation because most exist only in the shadowy places of our psyche. Eliminating them leaves us to deal with the real challenges that are out there somewhere, and we know that they can always be overcome because there is a solution to every problem if we're courageous enough to look for it.

In addition to dealing with negative perceptions and irrational thoughts, understanding our locus of control and expanding it in our minds helps us cope effectively and mobilize action. If we believe we are helpless—that nothing we do is likely to make a positive impact on our problems— we've created a self-fulfilling prophecy. In contrast, if we believe that we have the power to change our circumstances for the better, we move in the direction of possible solutions. We increase our chances of a positive outcome because, in dealing with adversity, doing something is always better than doing nothing. We see that glimmer of hope burn brighter with our actions, and our resolve strengthens as we build momentum for success.

In trying to cope with adversity and overcome obstacles to joy and fulfillment, we need to also acknowledge what is out of our control. The earth still turns and the tides ebb and flow no matter what we believe the nature of things is supposed to be. There are certain things that we just can't impact, no matter how hard we might try. Futile efforts to make it otherwise expend the precious physical and emotional resources that are best applied to the things you *can* control.

What you can't impact you must adapt to, so acknowledge where you must transform rather than try to move the immovable. That conserves your energies to focus on the circumstances you actually can impact. In other words, capture the rainwater and use it rather than trying to make it stop raining.

One of the areas you cannot exert influence over is *time*. If you live in the land of regret and constantly look behind you at the way things were 'supposed to be,' you forget to live for today. Likewise, life can be wasted dreaming of a better future rather than acting to make that future become reality. In *Personal Development for Smart People*, Steve Pavlina puts it this way: "There is no power in the past; the past is over and done with. There is no power in the future; the future exists only in your imagination. You have no power to act yesterday or tomorrow. Whenever you project beyond the present, you make yourself powerless because you're succumbing to an illusion. Consequently, it makes sense to focus your attention on the current moment since it's the only place you have any real power."[55]

- *Do you catch yourself in "crazy" and challenge your irrational thoughts about problems and their consequences?*
- *Do you use reframing to help you gain perspective so that you don't unnecessarily burn emotional energy by catastrophizing problems?*
- *Do you work to expand your locus of control when problems strike? Do you also acknowledge what is out of your control that you must adapt to?*

DEALING WITH REJECTION AND CRITICISM

People won't always say nice things about you. You won't be chosen for every job you desire, every school you want to get into, every sports team you wish to join, or every group where membership is coveted. Your love and attention won't always be returned, and the person who you've become infatuated with may not feel the same.

I know that explaining you will inevitably experience criticism and rejection probably doesn't make it sting any less for you when it happens. However, you have a choice about how you handle both. You can either let them define you, eroding your self-esteem and crippling your ability to respond constructively, or you can learn from them and use the experiences to bring you closer to fulfillment and your own sense of success.

Mark McGuiness, in his wonderful book *Resilience*, says, "If this were easy, everyone would do it. But everything has a price. If you want to achieve something extraordinary with your life, then rejection is a part of the price. Most people are not willing to pay that price … there are no guarantees—otherwise more people would be willing to persist. So you need to keep going in the face of uncertainty as well as rejection, and this puts you in an even smaller category."[56] The price of joy and prosperity is often failure, hardship, criticism, and pain on the journey. The first step in dealing with these things is to understand that nothing worth having ever comes easy and the path is often strewn with obstacles.

Your resolve will be tested. Rejection hurts. And it hurts because we identify the outcome of our efforts as an extension of ourselves. We believe our outcomes are part of *who we are*, rather than *something we did*. Because of this, when rejection occurs we believe that *we* are being rejected, *we* aren't good enough, *we* don't belong. We find it very difficult to separate what we do from who we are. Since affiliation is a basic human need, when we're told we don't belong in whatever group we aspire to, there's an empty place in us that needs filling.

As we continue with our discussion of criticism and rejection, remember: Thomas Edison was once asked by a reporter how it felt to fail *a thousand times*; Jack Canfield's work, *Chicken Soup for the Soul*, was rejected by *144* publishers; Tom Brady was drafted *199*[th] by the New England Patriots in 2000; Jack Ma, founder of e-commerce giant Alibaba, was rejected by Harvard *ten times* as well as from *every job* he applied to immediately after college.

Rejection is *one* person's perspective, shared with you at a moment in time, *about something you have done, not who you are*. Rejection and criticism are opinions, that's all. They are not the objective truth. We don't have to agree with them. In fact, when we start agreeing is when we stop progressing. Now this isn't to say that there aren't lessons to be learned from criticism and rejection. We should reflect on them long enough to learn from them, but they don't define you any more than not being picked first in the NBA draft defined Michael Jordan.

We have to consider the source when we experience rejection and criticism. When it comes from someone we respect and have a long-standing relationship with, we listen and take the feedback carefully into account. When it's someone with a reputation we admire but we don't know, we listen too. Everyone else gets placed in the proper perspective.

Of course, this isn't to say that strangers can't teach us something about ourselves, but we consider the feedback and the manner of the delivery as well as the source. Don't believe that every piece of negative information you receive about yourself is valid or valuable, because it's not. You have the power to determine that, and it must be a balancing act. Neither those who continually dismiss criticism and rejection nor those who blindly accept it all the time learn much about themselves.

In an effort to seek validation and significance, we sometimes overextend ourselves. We apply for membership to every group in which we have even a mild interest in the hopes that being accepted will feed our need for affiliation. We throw spaghetti at the wall to see what sticks, putting a bit of effort into each possible group rather than a lot of effort into just a few that we have enduring interest in. We play the numbers game. And in doing so, we are rejected more often.

The numbers game doesn't work in favor of your self-esteem. Instead of being told "No" a couple of times, you hear it more often. You need to be aware of the opportunities you chase to ensure they are really worth the prospect of rejection and are ones you truly value. Playing the numbers game only increases your chances of rejection because you underperform in relation to your potential for the opportunities you really wanted by wasting your talent and effort on those you didn't value much in the first place.

Where you had the talent to be accepted and were not because you didn't execute, you must acknowledge the rejection, learn from it, and apply your efforts more effectively next time. It then becomes about practice. Even if you felt that you did enough to warrant acceptance, there's no sense arguing about it; the decision's been made.

Have you ever seen a sports referee change a decision because a player complained about it? Neither have I. Move on from rejection and focus on a future opportunity rather than the past one that isn't going to happen. Whether your rejection is truly your loss or the other party's is irrelevant. Forge ahead. Thomas Edison said of his difficulties in inventing the light bulb, "I have not failed. I've just found 10,000 ways that won't work." Imagine if he had obsessed about the last time failure occurred. We might all be sitting in the dark right now!

I'm sure there have been times you didn't make the grade or have the required skill or experience. It happens, and you have to accept that there are ways you can improve your thoughts, actions, and experience to put yourself in a better position to succeed next time. You may also be the best performer out of a pool of people in one circumstance and the worst in another. In some ponds you can be the big fish, while in others you may be a minnow. As incremental success and progress helps build your self-esteem, you might decide on a smaller pond until your experience grows big enough to swim in the larger ones. Don't take on an Ironman competition when your training, skill, and experience has only prepared you for a sprint-distance race.

When rejection and criticism happen, we are an inherently biased participant who can easily lose perspective and become our own worst critic, sowing doubt and regret in our minds and eroding our sense of self-worth. No one can do damage to you without your permission—and that includes you. Your critical feedback isn't going to be balanced, proportional, or objective in the wake of criticism and rejection from the outside world.

The second-guessing and belittling you do to yourself means you've given yourself permission to slowly self-destruct. That's neither what you want nor intend, so flip the script mentally and show some self-compassion. Give yourself a break. Why would you want to pile on the misery by being unkind to yourself? Put it on a shelf and move on. There is no objective truth out there, only the realities you manufacture for yourself or allow others to create for you.

Perception *is* reality. Our thoughts lead to feelings, and our feelings lead to action (or inaction). The epitome of this is Henry Ford's comment: "Whether you think you can or think you can't, your right."

- *How do you react to rejection and criticism? How well do you believe you deal with them?*
- *When rejection and criticism occur, do you view them as an opinion or objective truth?*
- *Do you view rejection and criticism as being about* who you are, *or* something you did?
- *Do you make half-efforts with activities or groups that aren't important to you, increasing your chances of experiencing criticism or rejection?*
- *Are you your own worst critic when rejection or criticism occurs, or can you acknowledge and learn from it and move on?*

YOU ARE NOT ALONE...

A burden shared is a burden halved. Your resilience is supported and stress managed by connecting with others. Think of your network of friends, family, and colleagues as the repair service along life's journey. Occasionally your car breaks down and you don't have the means to fix it yourself. Perhaps you just need a jump start for the battery or a tow out of a ditch. Some people can even talk you through the problem, helping you figure out what is wrong with your car so you can fix it yourself and get back on the road.

There's a rescue service out there for each of us, even when our network of friends and family is small. Even if there's no one in it today, there are good Samaritans out there who are willing to become friends tomorrow and groups dedicated to helping others through tough spots. It's important to find those who can help validate your feelings and lend an ear and a shoulder to cry on from time to time.

Having compassionate, empathetic people in your life provides you crucial reassurance, instills belief and courage to overcome hardships, and offers people to stand beside you when adversity strikes. Find those people, lovingly cultivate and maintain those relationships, and be there for them in their own times of need. These people are a treasure, and you should treat them as such.

Reaching out to these people and talking through your challenges has a number of benefits. For one, others can call out your irrational, negative thinking. They can relay their own similar experiences to let you know that you're not alone in going through such challenges and that others have overcome them. They help you combat the temptation to isolate yourself by checking in on you and provide counsel to help put tough times in the rearview mirror. Connecting with others can also put your troubles in perspective, as you come to realize that others you know—or others they know—have been through seemingly far worse problems and have weathered them.

There are stories of triumph over tragedy everywhere, and they're easier to come across when you connect with others who can tell those tales. For a little inspiration, look up "Team Hoyt" online. The story of Dick Hoyt's loving support for his son, and both he and his son's support for others, is an emotional tale about difficult circumstances turned into triumph because of Rick and Dick's genuine care and compassion for others. It's likely that many have come across Rick and Dick by chance, and their lives have been brightened as a result.

There are Ricks and Dicks out there for each of us, acting as beacons when we find ourselves in dark places. It's better to know who they are before you begin to flounder, but if you're already in the midst of struggle you're going to have to seek them out. There are plenty of people willing to extend a hand if they just know who to hold it out to.

- *Who are those you trust to support you and talk through issues when you experience challenges?*

- *Do you use your support network to help you when you experience challenges and adversity, or do you isolate yourself?*
- *Do you use these people as resources to help call our your negative thinking and regain perspective on your challenges?*

TREAT YOURSELF RIGHT

In challenging times, you must ensure that you're doing your best to treat both your body and mind with kindness in order to maintain resilience and control stress. There have been numerous studies on the effects of lack of sleep on mood and they have concluded that there is a relationship between sleep deprivation and mood disorders such as anxiety and depression, as well as irritability, panic disorders, and increased stress. In addition, erratic behavior, psychotic episodes, and poor cognitive performance (e.g., slow decision-making, forgetfulness, increased errors) can be the result of sleeplessness.

During a time of adversity, the mental resources you need at your disposal to overcome obstacles can be drained by sleep deprivation. Anyone who has ever traveled with me when I've been awake for twenty-four hours or more can attest to the relationship between lack of sleep and mood swings, including me being generally irritable.

Research has also linked poor sleep to increased risk of obesity, heart disease, stroke, arthritis, and diabetes, as well as shortened life expectancy. High blood pressure, low sex drive, and weakened immune systems have also been associated with sleep deprivation.

In short, it's clear that the quality and quantity of our sleep affects us both physically and mentally. If you're looking to build resilience, control stress, and maintain good physical and mental health, sleep matters. Sleeping your life away can't really happen, as proper sleep can actually help you live longer. Long live Saturday afternoon naps!

Diet has also been studied in relation to stress and mental health (Of course, diet's relationship to physical health has been well documented too.). The effects of vitamin C on lowering cortisol (a stress hormone) have been studied, as well as the effects of complex carbohydrates such as whole grains, fruits, and vegetables on the production of serotonin (a mood-stabilizing hormone associated with feelings of pleasure and happiness).

There is a whole host of studies that link what we eat and drink to our stress levels and mental well-being, and it's worth noting that what we put in our bodies affects our minds too. We know about the negative effects of abusing substances like drugs and alcohol, both on our bodies and our minds, and we know that anything taken in excess is generally not good for us either. Watch what you reach for during times of stress and adversity since what you eat and drink can either become part of the problem or part of the solution.

Besides sleep and diet, exercise affects the production of endorphins, which are chemicals the brain uses to counteract stress and pain. This accounts for the runner's high, or feel-good factor, during physical exertion. Exercise can also serve as a distraction from the problems of the day, and like other forms of meditation or reflection allows us space and time to gain perspective on our challenges. The positive effect of exercise on mood elevation, decreased stress (associated with adrenaline, epinephrine, and cortisol levels), increased self-esteem, and improved sleep has also been studied. Exercise has been used to treat both depression and clinical anxiety. If you want to improve the ability of your mind, as well as your body, to help you weather tough times and remain resilient, the message is clear: get moving!

Many also find meditation and mindfulness exercises to be helpful ways to manage stress, control emotions, and calm the body and mind when adversity strikes. Meditation may have pain management benefits, help with sleep, and increase focus, self-awareness, and concentration. An increased ability to practice patience and tolerance and lower blood pressure are other potential benefits. In the previous section about emotional intelligence, I talked about the helpfulness of increasing the space between stimulus and our reaction. By slowing down and calming our bodies and minds, we may be able to take back control of our emotions and improve our perspective on our problems. This helps when we determine when and how to best deal with them.

So, eat, sleep, exercise, and treat your mind right. These were the things your mother probably reminded you of when you were young and your early education reinforced. It is actually quite good advice as it concerns your mental well-being, stress management, and ability to build and maintain resilience.

Sometimes the most basic and obvious advice is also the best. As the relationship between these things and your mood and mental well-being has been established, using them to manage your emotional responses and increase self-awareness is also emotionally intelligent.

- *Do you watch your sleep, diet, and exercise in order to prepare your mind and body to cope with life's challenges?*
- *Have you used mindfulness and meditation to help maintain your physical and mental health and cope with adversity? If not, would you be open to trying them?*
- *Do you have any unhealthy coping habits you use today (e.g., drugs, alcohol, self-blame, emotional outbursts)?*

REFLECTION AND RESULTS

There are times when you must slow down—or even stop. For those of us with restless feet who seem to be more comfortable in motion, this is difficult to do. But lack of motion doesn't mean lack of action. You need to think your way out of tough situations. Taking time to reflect on where you are, how you got here, and what options exist for resolving your problems is crucial. This isn't just stopping to allow random thoughts to pass between your ears; it's a purposeful exercise to assess your current situation, learn from it, and overcome hardships.

The first thing you must understand is where you are right now. What problems are occurring? What are their effects on you today and possibly tomorrow? How many are there? What are the priority issues to deal with? It's going to be hard but try to explore them like a detached observer. Use facts, not judgments. Assess what you see, hear, and feel—not the "why" of it all—right now. This doesn't mean that you're ignorant to the meaning you might draw from your current circumstances. It's just that when we're lost, the first thing we try to do is figure out where we are so we can then orient ourselves in the direction we want to go. Put a pin in your life map so you know where you're starting the next leg of your journey from.

Taking some time to figure out how you got to where you are can also be useful because the actions that led you into the problem are never those that lead you out of it. Beware though; there's an important difference between reflection and rumination. Rumination is attaching judgment. We've already spoken about self-compassion, and negative self-talk and self-blame do you absolutely no good here. They can be perilous for your self-esteem and confidence, weaken your resilience, and do absolutely nothing to help you solve your problems. Don't go there. It's a lot harder to find your way out of the land of regret than to travel into it. You need to conserve your time and emotional energy for the task at hand.

As Mark Samuel says in *Making Yourself Indispensable*, "The people succeeding make the same mistakes you do, but they skip self-judgment and move right to corrective learning and action. They don't waste time in self-pity or self-recrimination. They are focused only on solving the challenges before them."[57] If you assess how you came to be in your current situation without judging yourself, you can understand what actions may help you cope with your challenges and which will be counterproductive.

If you know that a flat tire caused you to drive into the ditch, then you don't waste time checking the brakes, which are working. You can also assess what you've learned about yourself by dealing with this situation and other difficulties in the past (Remember, *no* judgments, just an understanding of how you cope/behave.). If you know that certain people or situations cause you stress, avoid them if possible. There's no use adding to stress unnecessarily when coping with hardships.

Remember that others can also provide you with valuable feedback if they have witnessed you dealing with adversity and stress in the past. Don't rely on only your own insights if others can provide useful thoughts too. This can help you determine what solutions are most practical or best for you.

Having figured out where you are and how you got there, it's time to figure out where to go from here. This is about coming up with solutions and getting positive results. Come up with some ideas. You don't have to do this alone; your support network can provide ideas you may not have considered, as others will have a more detached perspective on your situation. When your problems seem insurmountable, you can eat the elephant one bite at a time. Break your problem down into manageable pieces and decide which are the most important to address first.

There's a reason that many workplace projects have milestones; they help break large, daunting initiatives into several objectives that can more easily be conquered. This is done for several good reasons. The first is to provide evidence of the payoff of hard work. It's nice to see that we're making progress. The act of setting and reaching goals provides focus and purpose to your efforts. Achievement also enhances self-esteem and feelings of control, both of which benefit your resilience.

If you're off track somehow, using milestones helps you alter your actions before you go too far in the wrong direction. If you are three degrees off course after a mile of travel, it's easy to get back on your intended path. After a hundred miles, it takes far more time and effort. In addition, when others see that you're making progress they, too, become encouraged and more vocal in their support. There's a reason that cheering fans line racecourses. They're shouting the participants toward the finish line. Once you decide on a course of action, get some fans if you can and begin your race.

The process of writing down our goals has been shown to improve the chances that we will actually follow through. It solidifies our commitment to ourselves, and when we discuss our goals with others, there's additional motivation to follow through in order to be true to our word.

So, setting and achieving goals helps you work your way out of hardship. Be kind to yourself. Make your goals small to begin with and set progressively more challenging goals as you begin to build up a record of success. You'll gain the confidence and momentum along the way to leap over the obstacles in front of you.

- *Is reflection currently part of the way you cope with challenges and adversity?*
- *Do you take the time to think about how to break down seemingly insurmountable problems so you can "eat the elephant one bite at a time"?*
- *Do you use goal setting as a means of navigating out of adversity and problems today?*

DEALING WITH CHANGE

The only constant in life is change, and the VUCA (Volatile, Uncertain, Complex, Ambiguous) world we live in seems to be getting only more VUCA each day. Less than a year ago, I couldn't have imagined that I'd be writing about change in the midst of one of the worst health pandemics of the century; one that has caused a global economic meltdown and significantly affected how we work, live, and travel.

As much as we'd like to think that by using our immense technical and scientific knowledge we can control the winds of change or even harness them in a predictable way, that just isn't the case. Change is the new normal, with periods of calm and stability occasionally happening in between. That has big implications for us. We must learn to be increasingly adaptable and find ways to cope constructively with change hitting us at a faster pace than ever before.

Change can cause an uneasy feeling to creep into the pit of our stomachs. It's a feeling of disorientation, where we search for something concrete to stand on rather than shifting sand. We long for the comfort of knowing that tomorrow will look similar to today—and that assurance no longer exists. It's been replaced by the reality that whatever we know, whatever we do, and whatever we are 'good' at today will become obsolete in the near future and we'll have to reinvent ourselves yet again. It's no wonder stress, absenteeism, and disengagement are widespread societal challenges.

But along with change comes opportunity. Risks can be both real and imagined, but there's potential for reward too.

Change offers incredible opportunity and challenge. Reinventing ourselves can be energizing and exciting. The learning and experience that accompany change are invaluable if you're open to the lessons. Renewal has great appeal, and people who navigate change effectively can thrive and grow while others struggle just to survive.

Dealing with change involves both emotions and process. You might say that *change* is a process that happens out there somewhere, in the external environment. The internal, emotional journey people go through in reaction to change is *transition*. William Bridges discusses this in more detail in his excellent book *The Way of Transition*, and the concept makes absolute sense. *Change* occurs out in the external world, progressing in its own way at its own pace. People and organizations can both plan for and implement change, but it's a process that's happening outside of the self. *Transition*, on the other hand, is internal and consists of our thoughts, emotions, and behaviors *in reaction to change*. It occurs in a different way, and often at a different pace, than change.

We've all known people who are quick to adapt to change in terms of their behaviors and emotions, as well as those who struggle and are slow to do so (if ever). *Change* can occur collectively, with many people being subject to it at the same time, but *transition* is an individual phenomenon. Everyone experiences it differently based on their own unique history and characteristics. There's no process map for transition and no one 'right' way - because the process of transition is experienced only by the self. By understanding more about the nature of change and transition, however, we can learn to use the resources and techniques that each of us finds most useful.

RESISTANCE TO CHANGE

Both at work and in our personal lives, people can communicate, embrace, resist, thrive in, or struggle with change. The environment may force change upon us, but humans drive a lot of change too. With the ever-increasing pace and overall levels of change, an air of change cynicism can pervade our lives. Fear can drive change resistance. The status quo has certain advantages in our minds, after all. It's the comfortable, predictable devil we know. The status quo may not be ideal—it may even be somewhat insane—but it's the crazy we know, and that has significant appeal.

Change is uncertain. Our transition journey isn't a path yet built or known, and we're unsure whether the promise of a better tomorrow that change *may* bring will ever really occur. The more insidious places of our psyche will fill in the blanks of an unknown story, often catastrophizing possible change outcomes.

The emotions we experience over uncertainty, loss of the familiar, and the pain that change may spark can all cause stress. An emotional loss can be felt too. When the status quo, which we're familiar with and 'good' at, is lost, our sense of self-esteem can decrease by having to start again as a novice in a new reality. We're attached to the current reality we helped build, after all. It can feel disheartening to have to start over due to changes in relationships, career, finances, or other life circumstances. We may feel threatened by change, and the more deeply affected by it we are, the more potential resistance we'll have simply because there's more at stake for us. Natural reactions include "fight or flight," where we either withdraw or we actively work against change. In both cases, our transition process stalls. These innate responses stem from the belief that anxiety and fear will subside if we can just avoid putting ourselves in the midst of change.

Another reason we resist change is denial. By fighting against change, we hope to avoid both accepting the unpleasant reality we're faced with today and looking in the mirror to admit our part in our current circumstances. Acknowledging our part means admitting that we may have made mistakes, hurt ourselves or others, and are at least partly accountable for the situation we find ourselves in. External forces may have brought hardship on us in some cases, but in many others we're the author of our own fate.

Admitting mistakes, mending fences, and acknowledging your responsibility for your circumstances can be painful, but it's also necessary if you want to alter them for the better. It means accepting, rather than denying, your current reality. Susan David, in *Emotional Agility*, writes about the fact that acceptance of your current circumstances is a prerequisite for making changes in your life.[58] You don't have to like your current situation; you just have to make peace with the fact that you are where you are and you can't control the universe. Make peace with the present, and yourself, and then you can concentrate on making changes for happiness and prosperity. As William Bridges explains, doing nothing leads you down a dangerous path.

> The refusal to change will not guarantee that whatever we care about stays the same. It only assures that whatever we care about has been deprived of the very thing it needs in order to survive. A marriage, a career, a dream for the future, even a picture of the past: Each of these things is being primed for destruction if it does not change over time. Here is another paradox: The very things we now wish that we could hold onto and keep safe from change were themselves originally produced by changes. And many of those changes, in their day, looked just as daunting as any in the present do. No matter how solid and comfortable and necessary the *status quo* feels today, it was once new, untried and uncomfortable.[59]

We would do well to remember that our lives are not a series of distinct events, unrelated to one another. Our current circumstances are the result of our personal evolution; transitions to the current state we cling to happened because of changes to some other status quo that we also cherished. It's just the way of things.

Loss is another reason change is resisted. French poet Paul Valéry said, "Every beginning is a consequence—every beginning ends something." Change has consequence for the present. It becomes lost to the past, and the attachment you have signals that you're going to feel some loss. Whether the loss is real or imagined, your thoughts fuel your emotions, and your emotions drive behavior.

For whatever we believe we stand to lose, we calculate the cost of change, and sometimes in our mind the price can become very, very expensive. Whether that price is all of the comforts, feelings, and benefits that come from a relationship or the prestige, familiarity, and financial reward of a current job, our minds often calculate loss before gain. This might include loss of love, respect, face, and membership in groups. Change can often seem complicated because one change rarely occurs independently of others. One change in our lives often triggers others, like falling dominos. Then we begin to multiply the losses in our heads.

The potential confusion and pain of change can also cause resistance. We think about the losses change might bring and worry about the uncertainty and whether the better tomorrow will actually occur. Our minds pile on the misery by considering the confusion and pain that *might* accompany change.

There's a state during change referred to as "the neutral zone" when you have let go of the status quo, which was comfortable, familiar, and perhaps something you were adept at, but you haven't yet come to grips with your new reality. The confusion and unease of being in this state can cause stress, and taxes your resilience. If you linger in the neutral zone too long or the discomfort is great, your emotional resources can't be used to make progress in your transition. You turn on survival mode instead, and transition stalls. "Fight or flight" then becomes the order of the day.

You might weigh the pain of the change in terms of the time and effort it takes to travel to your new reality. Having to acknowledge your present reality, take accountability for creating your current circumstances, and make the journey to make things 'right' again is also often calculated into the cost of change.

Everything I just talked about is likely playing out in your head, particularly if you're at the beginning or in the early stages of change. The fear, the pain, the loss—much, if not all of it, hasn't yet been realized and may never be. You're simply staging a battle between your ears at this point, finding reasons not to walk forward. With all of the *potential* issues, you have to remember that they're *illusions* and not reality. The future hasn't been written yet, and you don't possess the power to foretell the future—only to create it with what you do in the here and now.

- *What do you fear in respect to a change you are going through?*
- *Are your fears associated with uncertainty about what the future will look like after the change?*
- *What do you fear losing about the way things are today?*
- *What pain and confusion do you fear and believe might occur during the change?*
- *Are all your fears realistic, or are you out of perspective and thinking irrationally?*
- *What are the chances that these fears will actually be realized?*
- *What are the odds that the negative consequences of change will be as bad as you're imagining?*

RISK, BUT ALSO OPPORTUNITY

There are a variety of reasons people choose to embrace change rather than resist it. One of these is that change contains opportunities: to start new relationships and transform your current ones, to learn skills and take on challenges, to gain experience, reimagine yourself, and begin anew. The variety it brings to life can be deeply energizing. Renewal and innovation are exciting. You can wash away pain and strife and replace them with happiness and an improved self.

With a natural human focus on the negative, it's easy to forget the myriad of appeals change can hold. You don't have to discard your past on some mental trash heap, unless you determine that's the best way to constructively move forward. After all, the past has gotten you where you are today. Maybe the situation isn't ideal, but you're alive and breathing! One thing the global health pandemic did was remind many of us to be grateful for what we have rather than constantly focusing on what we lack. You can pay homage to the past while acknowledging that you must move on in order to make today and tomorrow brighter.

Now being grateful for what led you to today doesn't mean you have to cling to it. Without changing you can't grow, after all. As William Bridges eloquently says in *The Way of Transition*, "One thing that the reorientation function doesn't account for is that in reorienting ourselves, we also have the chance—although it is optional whether or not we seize it—to take a step forward in our own development by letting go of a less-than-adequate reality and an out-of-date self-image. So the second function of transition is *personal growth*."[60] The wonderful thing about change is that you get to choose what you learn from it—and how you learn. Your attitude toward change determines how much value you'll derive from it as you transition to a new reality.

Consider the changes you're undergoing. There may be opportunities to forge new loves, friendships, and networks that are not only exciting but can also help you feel significant, provide you emotional support and group affiliation, and help you learn and grow. Different contacts mean new possibilities. The opportunities to work alongside new people, in new jobs, and on different projects can be great learning experiences, and you draw your own lessons from change too. If *wisdom = knowledge + reflection*, then gaining new knowledge through change offers the potential for greater wisdom.

For example, living in new places exposes us to different cultures, where we can broaden our minds, expose ourselves to diversity, and gain further appreciation of both commonalities and differences among people. New surroundings often provide us excitement too and the chance to experience history and explore new corners of the world. We build memories and friendships that far outlast our bank account balances. We can build legacies, making a positive impact on both ourselves and those around us through such life changes.

Progress and growth are basic human needs and are, by definition, changes. You can't accomplish them sitting on the sidelines. Change resistance can also be exhausting. It's like swimming against a river's current to get to the shore. By understanding that fighting the flow of change only makes you exhausted and at risk of drowning, you can decide to shape your fate. There's still a way to get to shore, although it may be downstream a bit. You have the choice of which riverbank you land on and can always hike back up to your destination—if you decide you still want to get there.

- *Think about the changes you are currently going through or considering implementing:*
- *Are you open to the potential that there will be benefits from it?*
- *What is positive or exciting about it?*
- *What opportunities are there for learning and personal growth?*
- *Are there chances to build new relationships and support networks?*
- *What new experiences might lie ahead for you?*
- *What will the valuable parts of this change be for you?*

KEEPING CHANGE IN PERSPECTIVE

We've all thought our world was turned upside down at some points in our lives until some sage person helped us understand that the earth was still round and the sun still rose and set each day.

Guard against losing perspective during change, thinking that everything is changing and adding unnecessarily to your emotional baggage and stress. Let yourself become grounded in what remains the same before you consider the things you used to do that will now stop or how things will be different in the future.

It's important to understand what you can influence and what you can't in order to cope with change, By doing so, you can focus your finite time, attention, and energy on changes you can affect rather than wasting effort on those you can't. The sun rises in the east every day and sets in the west. The tides ebb and flow. Health pandemics occur. These and other things in your life you can neither influence nor control, so you must choose to either accept this reality and adapt or deny it and struggle.

Identifying and accepting what you cannot change is a crucial part of coping successfully. By adapting to what you can't control, you can then focus your efforts on the things you can impact. As Ryan Holiday states in *The Obstacle is the Way*, "In its own way, the most harmful dragon we chase is the one that makes us think we can change things that are simply not ours to change … Focusing exclusively on what is in our power magnifies and enhances our power. But every ounce of energy directed at things we can't actually influence is wasted—self-indulgent and self-destructive. So much power—ours, and other people's—is frittered away in this manner."[61]

Change is a regular part of our life experience, whether in our personal lives or the workplace. It's the reality we all deal with today. Whether change is structured and planned, or is something unexpected, you must react to it. If you're going to thrive—not just survive—you've got to understand what concerns you have about change. You need to address those concerns and seize the opportunities to positively impact your life with change. You are not static; born fixed and preprogrammed, never to transform and grow. The story of our lives isn't chiseled in stone, with some predestined to be leaders or smarter and better than the rest. That's a myth insecure egotists perpetuate.

There is greatness, joy, and prosperity in you. You're a person of unbelievable potential. Remember, you write the narrative of your own life, and successfully handling change helps you craft it in the way you intend despite adversity, setbacks, and unexpected events.

SEEKING BEAUTY AND BALANCE

When adversity strikes we find our stress levels increasing, and when the winds of change howl around us, we all need a place of refuge now and again. There are likely to be places, times, and happenings that bring us consistent happiness. They represent the beauty in our lives. You've likely had some of these experiences with loved ones, who may or may not be around to help you repeat them in the future. You have also undoubtedly experienced being alone. Even when you're with others, you view experiences differently than they do, so a place or time that was incredibly special or happy for you may not have been so for others. But you know what those moments of happiness are for you, and they can be useful resources as you weather the occasional storms in your life.

For my part, I have a number of "happy places" I can go in my mind to recapture joy and contentment. My childhood was happy, and I've had a very loving and supportive family. I was fortunate to spend summers at a family lake home, where I swam, fished, and spent a lot of time on the water in a canoe or boat. I remember seeing the spectacular northern lights one night while fishing. And walking through a sea of monarch butterflies on the dirt road behind the cabin. I can still smell the lavender bushes in the field by my grandparents' home there too. I remember spending time gardening with my mother and grandfather. There were numerous family holidays there, including spectacular summer holiday parades and fireworks celebrations in the area.

Now I'm not a good gardener—anyone who knows me will likely tell you that. Gardening requires continual care and nurturing that I don't pay attention to well in the garden—or, at times, in my personal life. I do enjoy the beauty of a flower garden, however, and always enjoyed helping my own family tend to them. My talent may have been limited to digging holes and planting, but I liked spending time there with those I loved.

I can still envision both the Savill Garden and Virginia Water areas just west of London, and the peace I found wandering through these beautiful places. I've often taken quick vacations in my mind to the Lake District and Isle of Wight in England, and to Kauai, Prague, London, Croatia, Singapore, and other places I found beautiful and special—and the people I shared those experiences with. England is littered with picturesque villages, full of history and beauty that I always marveled at. I took advantage of it whenever I could.

I'm a runner (Not a fast one!), but I do get out regularly to run as a means not only of keeping fit but helping me cope with stress and challenges. I do get the "runner's high" that seems to make me feel generally more positive, and it allows me a little reflection time. I try other forms of exercise too in order to accomplish the same feelings. I also like to get out on my motorcycle, which is a hobby that keeps my mind occupied. I'm sure you have some hobbies and leisure interests too.

While some of the people I shared memories with may no longer be around, I get to replay my happiness again and again. Some call it nostalgia, but whatever the label we put on it, I feel better as a result. I hold no special powers to do this, and I'm sure you have the ability to use special people, places, and events in your life to rekindle joy whenever it is most needed. Whether it's a walk out to the local park, revisiting the greatest moments of happiness in your life, or the images of wonder and beauty projected from your mind's eye, you have the ability to take heart from them and stave off despair.

The other issue to consider, as it concerns resilience and stress management, is balance. There are certainly instances when I have not been a model of balanced living, and the times I was most imbalanced became real problems for myself and others. Balance can certainly mean something different for each of us; however, we all can relate to having an excess of certain elements in our lives and a lack of attention to others that may cause problems.

For example, do you "work to live" or "live to work?" Many of us, including myself, have become caught up in our careers at one point or another. Normally well-intentioned, a focus on your job can help you provide for yourself or your family, find meaning and significance, or fulfill needs for affiliation and acceptance. But these motivators can quickly lead to a lack of attention to other parts of our lives. We might stop paying as much attention to our health and well-being, our relationships, or the pursuit of other activities that bring us happiness.

For my part, what started as a well-intentioned desire to provide for my family and meet financial obligations, as well as a genuine interest in my profession and a need for professional acceptance, became unhealthy. My family moved perhaps more than most as I progressed my career, and those moves certainly resulted in trials and hardships for my spouse and children—who were nevertheless supportive. In one instance, the regular fear of losing my job and having to move the family yet again caused me to put in long and irregular hours to cling to my position.

While other drivers played a part too, I certainly did not want to fail, force my family to relocate again, and feel like I was unable to provide properly for their needs. In the end, however, this imbalance in my life caused me to focus too little on friends, family, and my own well-being, and that had a real negative impact on the health of some of my relationships (both with myself and others). I was not as good a friend, spouse, or father as I ideally wanted to be, and that is my greatest regret. Remember, time and tide cause us all to stop drawing breath at some point, and few regret what they may or may not have done with their career and money when the end comes.

You also need to balance attention on yourself with a focus on others—whoever they may be. Even the most well-meaning and selfless among us still need to attend to our own physical health and mental well-being, so ignoring the physical aches and emotional pains that arise is not sustainable. We've likely all been close to someone who has been devastated by physical illness or emotional issues. Some of them may have even taken their own lives, which is the ultimate tragedy. I don't want you to suffer something that may have been preventable while friends, family, and health professionals are available to help support you. Sometimes imbalance in your life is the cause of these problems, and other times it's something more. I wish a happy and healthy life for you, and where balance can help you, please make it a part of your life.

Check up on yourself. Make time to tend to your physical and mental wellness. Take it from someone who has learned the benefits of doing so—and consequences of ignoring it. It's vital. Remember, too, that the time you spend on yourself in those places of beauty and leisure interests are part of the balance you must seek in your life. Just as with resilience and stress management in general, tending properly to nutrition, exercise, rest, and mindfulness are all important as you balance how you treat yourself. Carving out time for some peace and fun never hurts! Do you set aside time for peace and fun, or are those the first things to be sacrificed when life gets busy?

Don't continually prioritize the minor things in your life—whatever they may be. By allocating time in a more balanced fashion among the things you hold dear, you'll find more enduring happiness. Only you will know what those precious things will be, according to your principles and values. When your life falls out of balance with them, you will know. The physical and emotional triggers will be there—so don't ignore them.

The quality and quantity of relationships can also be an issue of balance that must be addressed. Do you cultivate and nurture relationships properly today, providing them the attention needed? If so, do you have a variety of relationships with friends and family who can provide you a network of support when times are tough, or are there only one or two special people in your life? In such cases, what if that relationship breaks up, or the friendship ends? Will you be left with no one to turn to? Are you aware of the other support services that exist for you when physical or mental health issues occur? It's better to know ahead of time than be scrambling for help when you need it most.

The point is that balance in relationships can be important too. As I mentioned previously, I'm not suggesting a vast array of superficial acquaintances, but I am advocating for enough *quality* relationships that provide you happiness and support when you need it most. You, in turn, will seek to be a good friend, partner, parent, child, or sibling and provide others help and hope when they need it.

Most people are interested in *something* outside of their work. Those leisure interests provide you significance, affiliation, purpose, meaning, personal growth, or some other benefit. Relying on a variety of sources to help meet such needs can also help you remain resilient and happy. If you only have your motorcycle club rides, for example, and a health pandemic strikes that prevents people from getting together, what alternative pursuits do you have to help meet your needs? This is not, of course, a hypothetical problem since the recent health pandemic.

Work and play. Self versus others. The relationships you tend to and interests you pursue. Physical and mental health awareness. These are all questions of balance, and in a world where destructive fanatical behavior and obsession is often mistaken for dedication and focus, it's easy to fall out of balance and depart from your intended life path. I know—I've experienced it, and you have likely done so too at some point in your life. When the tires on your life's car fall out of balance, you run off the road sooner or later. Check them regularly by assessing the state of balance in your life, and you won't experience a crash.

- *What are beautiful memories you can call upon for strength? What people, places, and events have brought you joy that you can envision right now to lift your mood and help you cope with today's difficulties?*
- *Are there hobbies or interests you can undertake today that make you happy and distract you from ruminating over adversity and setbacks?*

- *Are there places you periodically go to find peace and relaxation and find a bit of beauty in your life?*
- *Do you use exercise or meditation today as tools to help lift your mood and cope with life's challenges? If not, would you be open to trying them?*
- *Is there balance in your life generally, where your time and attention are allocated to more than one pursuit (family, career, leisure, travel, exercise, friends, etc.)?*
- *Is there balance in the resources you use to remain resilient and cope with stress? Or do you rely on just one or two tools?*

Section Four

MANAGING RELATIONSHIPS

The most important relationship you establish and maintain is the one with yourself. You are strong and capable enough to handle your life journey, including the obstacles in the road. You have been your own rock and fortress, and you will continue to be. When you're comfortable in your own skin and enjoy your own company, the contentment you gain is a blessing. There's a difference between self-love and the infatuation with self that narcissists display. When you truly love yourself, you stop looking for someone else to complete you. The relationships you forge with others satisfy some basic human needs but making you a whole being shouldn't be one of them. You are good enough already.

When you reach the state of being fundamentally happy with yourself, which many of us continue to work toward, relationships with others become gifts you give yourself. Some relationships are professional and satisfy certain needs and drives, while others are mainly for love and enjoyment. All add richness to a life already whole.

When you do go looking for additional relationships, or others find you, there are some things you can do to build and maintain them constructively.

In *EQ Applied*, Justin Bariso defines relationship management as the ability to get the most out of your connections.[62] Bariso also mentions that relationship management includes the emotional benefits you provide to others and he talks about how trust strengthens personal bonds over time.

The idea that relationship management includes trust, investment, building rapport, and influencing others is important. In addition, the abilities to constructively manage interactions with challenging personalities and handle conflict effectively will help you build and maintain healthy relationships.

I'm not a relationship guru. I've had missteps with personal and professional relationships over a lifetime, and I certainly do not have all the answers. I think even the relationship experts will tell you that they've made their own fair share of relationship mistakes, however. Hopefully what you find in this exploration is that you can avoid some of the hard relationship lessons learned by others, including me.

YOU HAVE TO INVEST

It's been said that you don't get more out of a relationship than you put into it. In the short-term, strictly speaking, that's just not true. We've probably all experienced relationships in which we put a lot into it and received very little in return or put little into it and benefitted disproportionately. I agree with the sentiment overall, though, because time becomes the great relationship equalizer in the long-term. People are basically good and smart creatures, and when they see that they are investing far more than they're receiving, they do what any rational person would and turn their attention elsewhere.

There's a basic principle of reciprocity in relationships—a give and take—where both people come to the party with something of benefit and provide it to each other. Sometimes it's done consciously, but most of the time it's implicit. You have to prove you can add value to someone's life. It's that simple whether it's a personal or professional relationship. As Mark Sanborn says in *The Fred Factor*, "People are flattered when you express an interest in getting to know them better, not out of morbid curiosity, but in an effort to help or serve them more effectively."[63] It might be the time, attention, love, knowledge, or experience you give that positively impacts others. But like any good guest, don't show up for the party empty-handed. You won't be asked back if you do.

Bear in mind that your level of investment is going to vary. There's no cookie-cutter formula for relationships; no foolproof template. There's a wondrous thing about people: no two are exactly alike. Everyone comes into relationships with a unique combination of values, experience, knowledge, beliefs, hopes, and fears, and you're going to need to invest in order to even find out whether you can positively impact someone else and they in turn can add value to your life.

Now this isn't a transactional calculation where both people ask, "So, what have you got?" That would be a depressingly dark perspective on relationships. We do, however, determine whether being around others is generally enjoyable, makes us feel good about ourselves and our life, and makes us better for having known them. We simply make a decision based on what we think and feel. We rarely stop to consciously consider the costs and benefits of relationships; we just continue on if our heart and head tell us that it seems like a good idea.

I'm not denying that plenty of people become entrenched in relationships which are, in the end, not a good idea at all, and they remain in relationships despite their negative impact and other risks. People treat you exactly how you allow them to; however, sometimes fear, emotional control, hardship, and other forms of abuse cause us to remain in bad situations.

If this is happening to you, I'm sorry. You deserve better, and I hope you find the help and courage to break free of your situation.

The answer to whether you can change another person, by the way, is no. The only person you can change is yourself. While you can plant the seed of change in others, if they don't water it, nothing will happen. If the seed you planted doesn't take root in their heart, the soil where you've planted it in just isn't fertile. Perhaps you need to find new ground.

There's another thing to bear in mind about investing in relationships. Consider whether you are wise investing all your time, energy, and resources into just one or a couple of them. This is the all-eggs-in-one-basket approach. If you've ever been in love, then you've certainly experienced throwing your entire heart and soul into another. You thought of them constantly. Lived for them. Spent your nights dreaming of them when they weren't around.

Love is an absolutely wonderful thing (or any close friendship for that matter), but there's something to be said for balance. When you define your identity and sense of self-worth by the thoughts and feelings of only a small group—or even just that one special person—you place your heart and soul at great risk. Life's meaning, and your worth, become a roller-coaster ride that depends on the emotions of others. That's not a great place to be.

So, consider how you invest in your relationships and whether building them up with a few others who offer enjoyment and support—rather than just one or two—might help you experience less emotional mountains and valleys.

Don't be too tentative. When you do decide that a relationship is worth investing in, invest! It's better to make the effort and not see the return than to regret a half-hearted effort. Fortune favors the brave. You don't have to be blind to the risks or ignore the red flags that tell you to slow down and take stock of how things are going in the relationship, but it's better to make the effort to build a few close, trusting relationships than have a number of superficial relationships. As with most things in life, it's about quality over quantity in the end.

There is one relationship you need to prioritize above all others, however, and that is the relationship you have with yourself. I know, right now you are thinking, "How do I have a relationship with myself? That's ridiculous!" Just keep an open mind for the rest of this section.

Let's start by asking: How do you treat yourself? Do you make a positive impact on your own life, or do your thoughts, feelings, and actions detract from your happiness and prosperity? Do you invest time, resources, and attention in your physical and mental well-being, or do you neglect yourself? Are the conversations you have with yourself positive, supportive, and uplifting, or do they have the opposite effect? Can you be content in your own company, or are you always seeking someone else? During difficult circumstances, are you a source of your own emotional support, or do you abandon yourself?

As you can clearly see, you *do* have a relationship with yourself.

Invest in that relationship. You will always have one with yourself; it's the one relationship you cannot shed. From cradle to grave, you must live with yourself, and you have one chance at life. Make sure you take care of yourself.

Like any other relationship, you need to figure out how to nurture the relationship with yourself. Reflect on what your needs and desires are and what fears and flaws you hold. Explore your principles, values, and priorities. Consider your strengths and when you are most happy.

We all know there are things we can do to make ourselves content and support our desires. There are also times we can be our own worst enemy. This is why self-awareness is such a critical component of emotional intelligence and building relationships. Until you can become your own best friend, you can't possibly hope to become someone else's.

An important aspect of relationship investments is *selflessness*. We all hope to benefit from our relationships at some point, but relationships are not a business deal. They are not a transaction, and those who treat them as such miss out on the true benefits of connecting with others. They also risk being on the wrong end of the transaction when others decide a bigger, better deal lies elsewhere. Transactions are a cynical way to approach connecting with others and won't do much to support our true happiness and needs for care, affection, emotional support, and significance.

Be there for someone else; provide them support without expecting anything in return. Just do the right thing. It takes very little time to impact someone else positively, and your day is often filled with brief interactions in which you can have an impact. We build trust—and relationships—by giving of ourselves simply because we can and we know we can make a difference for someone else.

Give without expectation and you'll find the blessing is returned to you with a dividend of close, positive relationships and maintenance of your self-esteem. 'Good' people are generous, not always in the quantity of time they spend with any one person, but in the attitude they have about giving of themselves to support others. Generosity is often measured in minutes, not hours. But if it does take longer than minutes and you're in a unique position to help brighten someone else's life, consider doing so.

Investment in relationships means focusing on others' interests, not your own. Dale Carnegie famously said, "You can make more friends in two months by becoming interested in other people than you can in two years by trying to get other people interested in you." This means making a true effort to find out what others' needs are and whether you can support them somehow. If you can do that and deliver for others, they will do the same for you. It may not happen on an individual level, but in the aggregate, you will find that others will return your selflessness with selfless acts of their own. It's simply relationship karma.

Time and attention are the chief currencies of building relationships—not money and things. When you give of your time and attention, both of which are finite, others know and appreciate that sacrifice. These are precious resources, and others acknowledge when you spend them in order to help. Time and attention satisfy others' need for significance and demonstrate your commitment to building relationships and supporting others. Ask any person in the twilight of their lives and they will tell you, even if they're sitting on a pile of money and vast material wealth, that their regrets are connected to how and who they spent their time and attention on. These are the great equalizers. Every one of us has the same amount to give, and no one lies on their deathbed wishing they had more money in their bank account that they will not live to spend.

- *Are you a fair-weather friend, only taking and not giving, or do you consciously try to add something to each relationship you're in?*
- *Are you measured in how you invest in relationships, cultivating a few close connections, or do you pour your heart and soul into just one or two?*
- *Do you prioritize giving your time and attention (not money and things) when investing in relationships?*
- *Do you give without the expectation of receiving something back, or do you treat relationships like business transactions? Do you focus on others' interests or your own?*

TRUST'S ROLE

There's nothing novel about the concept that good relationships are built on trust. That's what experience has, sometimes painfully, taught us. From successful marriages and close friendships to the battlefield, boardroom, and sports field, when relationships are supported by mutual trust, everyone benefits and great things occur—love, enjoyment, success, fulfillment, happiness, and achievement. Name one successful human endeavor that was not built on trust. I can't, because even in individual accomplishments, people have built a relationship with themselves that includes trust. We trust in ourselves, and there's no better foundation to build a relationship on than trust.

When skepticism and manipulation enter into the fray, potential is lost. In the end, the relationship is almost certainly destroyed too. Lack of trust causes us to interpret bad intent from others' words and actions, to assume things are said and done to take advantage of us somehow. We read selfishness into the narrative of the relationship—and when we do so, we, in turn, become selfish in order to protect ourselves.

The instinct to protect ourselves is a natural human reaction, but one that hinders building relationships. Instead of turning our attention to how we can benefit others, our mind becomes obsessed with trying to figure out others' end games—what they are seeking to take from us by what they say and do. We create intrigue where none exists, our defensiveness shows, and others then become defensive too. This increases the chances that we're going to treat the relationship as transactional—a quid pro quo—rather than the organic give and take that healthy relationships have where no one keeps score.

I'm not advocating for you to dive into the deep end of every relationship with both feet. We all use our knowledge, experience, and instincts to decide how quickly, and how much, to invest in relationships. It's completely natural and understandable not to blindly trust everyone we come across. That would be foolish. We all have to protect our hearts, minds, and bodies and decide when it's safe to take leaps of faith.

The process of building trust isn't typically that dramatic; it's normally incremental. It's just important to be aware of the natural human tendency toward defensiveness. We may read manipulation into situations instead of assigning benign intent to others' words and actions until they prove otherwise. This can be a barrier to building trust and, ultimately, to close relationships.

If you're to build trust, you have to start with *integrity*. I've talked about integrity as being part of character, and others will assess both your character generally and your integrity specifically when deciding how, or if, to approach a relationship with you. We all assess the honesty of others when deciding whether to continue interacting with them. Will we be told the truth? We all know that relationships built on lies aren't real and never last. In contrast, there's great comfort in knowing that you will be dealt with honestly, and you will repay that honesty in kind if you, too, are a person of integrity.

The trust gained through integrity can be strong. Likewise, the trust broken by a breach of integrity is extremely hard to rebuild—if it can be repaired at all. As you can't, and shouldn't, put a price on your own integrity, make sure you are aware of the harsh consequences of deceit in your relationships. When we suspect dishonesty in others, we approach them with skepticism. This leads to a destructive spiral in which the negative intent we assign to each other's words and deeds causes miscommunication and conflict, often dooming the relationship.

Self-serving manipulation, while not our conventional definition of dishonesty, is also a breach of trust that puts your integrity at risk. You risk your integrity when you fail to be forthright and transparent about your intent. In such cases you commit a lie of omission by not disclosing how your request or another's words or actions are beneficial to your interests—whether or not they benefit others too.

When people find out that you've manipulated them for your own gain and told them half-truths, they'll feel used and take a dim view of your character. Others will eventually determine that your relationship with them is based on your interest in personal gain and that you're willing to covertly manipulate them on order to achieve that. The relationship is reduced to one that's very transactional and quid pro quo in nature at best and, at worst, it ends badly.

Transparency is an important aspect of trust. When you varnish the truth and withhold critical feedback—the stuff that stings but is ultimately the most useful—people learn that you're willing to spare their feelings and your discomfort at the expense of honesty. They learn that you're diplomatic and kind but not completely trustworthy. And if you can't be trusted about one thing, can you be trusted about anything?

Of course, I don't recommend brutal, undiplomatic truth that needlessly tramples others' feelings—but having the courage to provide the real and whole truth to someone, delivered in a manner that evidences your benign intent and care for others' interests, ought to gain you trust and respect in the end. This depends on the emotional intelligence of the person receiving your feedback, but you'll feel better knowing that you provided it with others' best interests at heart and were trustworthy and selfless. You were selfless because you provided feedback, putting yourself at risk for another's benefit when you had little or nothing to personally gain. As Daniel Goleman states in *Emotional Intelligence*:

> Another, perhaps more crucial kind of self-monitoring seems to make the difference between those who end up as anchorless social chameleons, trying to impress everyone, and those who can use their social polish more in keeping with their true feelings. That is the capacity to be true, as the saying has it, "to thine own self," which allows acting in accord with one's deepest feelings and values no matter what the social consequences. Such emotional integrity could well lead to, say, deliberately provoking a confrontation in order to cut through duplicity or denial—a clearing of the air that a social chameleon would never attempt.[64]

Here Goleman is speaking not just about transparency but also about *authenticity*. Many of us go through life trying to find ourselves and be comfortable in our own skin. Our ability to represent our true selves—with our words and actions reflecting our values, principles, and beliefs—is a critical aspect of emotional intelligence that also benefits our relationships.

There's genuine emotional tension within us when what we say and do are at war with how we really feel. The internal conflict is real and can be serious. In order to go along, get along, and fit in, we say and do things that conflict with our foundation, and that foundation weakens as a result. You lose respect for yourself, and when others find out you don't really believe in what you say and do, they also lose respect and trust for you.

There's another benefit to practicing authenticity for trust and building relationships. When you say when you mean and mean what you say, others see that your words and deeds are consistent with what you profess to believe. Trust comes as a result because thoughts, feelings, beliefs, and actions mutually support one another. You're seen as a person of conviction, of character. Now this doesn't mean that your beliefs are right or that they are superior to anyone else's, but it does mean that others can count on you to speak and act predictably based on your values and beliefs. And that builds trust.

As an authentic person, you will find your crowd more quickly. You don't waste precious time putting up and maintaining facades that conflict with your belief system just to fit in. Because of this, people will take you at face value, and you can take comfort in knowing that you're being judged and accepted based on who you really are—not just a shadow you're portraying in order to conform and be liked. This is deeply satisfying because your relationships are based on a portrayal of your authentic self, and you're being dealt with on that basis. This is what it's *truly* like to fit in, and it's a breath of fresh air. It's a great feeling to know you are—and always were—good enough and that you're accepted for just being you. If others can embrace your authentic self, that's wonderful. If not, just keep looking for your crowd.

Being authentic and a person of integrity will help you immensely as you build and maintain relationships. In addition, *credibility* counts. We often think of credibility in a business context. It's certainly true that in the workplace your credibility being able to perform your role and positively contribute to your organization affects your relationships. You build and maintain your credibility at work through competently carrying out your job and proving to be reliable, knowledgeable, and experienced. You build a track record of delivering quality work and impacting others positively.

In the rest of your life, building credibility isn't as formal, but it's no less important. Have you ever had—or been—the fair-weather friend who is fun at parties but can never be counted on when others need advice and support? Your reliability and responsibility are part of character too. When you can be counted on to do the things that need doing, including helping others, before doing the things you'd like to do, you demonstrate dedication to your relationships. Being there for others demonstrates selflessness. You build a track record of being someone who can truly be relied upon if life goes sideways and others need a helping hand, a sympathetic ear, or a shoulder to cry on. That's credibility. It's also doing what's plainly right and decent.

Credibility also increases when you prove to others that you're a reliable source of information and advice. When people come to you for help and you demonstrate wisdom through the quality of your counsel, they are positively impacted. And when you build a reputation as someone who helps others weigh their decisions in a thoughtful, considered way, you'll build the credibility that helps your relationships too.

Whether it's in work or our personal lives, we all assess how far and how fast to invest in relationships based partly on the credibility of others. When we can count on people to be consistent and reliable in what they say and do—including being there to support us just as we must commit to do for them—we're more likely to further our relationships with them. This is why, in the end, fair-weather friendships always fade away. Instead, be a lighthouse beacon for others when the weather closes in and their seas get rough.

Have you ever shared information in confidence, trusting that others will guard it as you asked and been disappointed? Have you experienced a time when another person was friendly and complimentary to your face, then found out that they were speaking negatively about you to others when you weren't around? Discretion is a component of trust that can be make or break for many relationships. When others share information in confidence, uphold their trust by treating it with care and discretion.

Now, this doesn't apply if situations come up when you have to weigh a betrayal of confidence against protecting the safety of someone else, upholding the law, or being consistent with your values and principles. We've all run across these kinds of hard decisions at one point or another. But barring those situations, honor the trust others place in you when they share information in confidence.

In addition—and related to both authenticity and discretion—ensure you are seen as a person with one face, not two. Two-faced people can swiftly destroy trust and relationships in a way that may be irreparable. Once trust is shattered by negative gossip and backstabbing, it's very hard to pick up the pieces and rebuild relationships into something resembling constructive. If you have an issue with someone, approach them and clear the air; don't pollute it with passive-aggressive, backstabbing behavior. When you are clear and direct with people about where you stand, your relationship is built on firm ground. Expect that courtesy of yourself, and of others, and the bonds of trust in your relationships will only strengthen.

- *Do you use honesty, transparency, and integrity to build trust in your relationships? Do you avoid manipulation and gossip?*
- *Can people count on you to do what you said you'd do, when and how you said you'd do it? Are you reliable?*
- *Do you use discretion and keep confidences as a means of building and maintaining trust?*
- *Do your words and actions truly reflect your values and beliefs?*

BUILD RAPPORT!

No relationship is built overnight. Even if the heavens collide and rockets go off in your heart, what you have is lust and infatuation, not a relationship. You like what you see and hear, but at this point, the pool is broad and shallow, not deep and substantive. In the business world, we're more likely to have admiration rather than lust but there, too, beware of falling in love with a candidate or colleague who sounds good in an interview and dresses the part but has not proved themselves yet. Real rapport isn't instant. Yes, first impressions matter. That's why we all preen and flex in the mirror, and worry about our dress and appearance. Those things can make a difference in getting you noticed—that's just the reality of human nature.

Remember, though, that we're all beautiful to somebody. There's someone waiting for the perfect version of their soulmate, father, mother, son, daughter, friend, coworker, boss, or teammate. That person is in the mirror. Take it from a gangly six-foot-eight-inch tall guy who will never win a body-building contest or grace the cover of *Vogue*. I spent my youth trying to fit in and my adult life trying to (metaphorically speaking!) stand out. It's taken a lot longer than I expected to be comfortable with my reflection, understanding that the person whose opinion matters the most is waiting in the mirror. I have to be content with who I am, and so do you. We all try to be the best versions of ourselves that we can *on any given day*. If you're comfortable that's happening and you are content with the path you've chosen, if others can't accept you for who you are then find new surroundings.

Now, the *surface* reflection in the mirror does matter when it comes to getting noticed. We all look beyond that, however, when we stare into the mirror. After others notice the surface reflection, it is up to you—and them—to see if the relationship blossoms in time by building *rapport*. Rapport is about what's underneath the first impressions and is the *true* heart of healthy relationships. It's about feelings first, then thoughts and ideas—not about looks and first impressions.

Our lives are dominated by emotion. We're feeling something every minute of our waking day, whether we acknowledge it or not. Acknowledging the power of emotion in our lives, Carl W. Buechner said, "They may forget what you said, but they will never forget how you made them feel."

So, when you build rapport and a *real* relationship, you build them on feelings. Anyone who keeps staring at the surface rather than worrying about what's on the inside has already determined for you that they're not the right person to be building a close relationship with.

THE REALITY OF IMPRESSIONS

Having just emphasized that true rapport and building relationships are about substance over form, I'm going to talk about impressions for a minute. They matter. That's the bottom line. Substantial research on the subject indicates that others form initial opinions of you very quickly—in a couple of minutes or less—based on your interactions with them.

Unfair? Undoubtedly. Reality? Absolutely.

There's an old adage that says "You never get a second chance to make a first impression," and there's a reason for this. People like to be right. Frankly, it's more comforting to be right all the time than be wrong periodically. Ask any hardcore egotist.

In fairness, most of us feel the same way—at least to a degree. This is why there's a natural bias for interpreting information in order to confirm our initial impressions rather than dispute them. Ego lurks in the background, pointing us in the direction of information that tells us we were right all along. This is precisely why you don't reach for that pizza with onions and garlic bread before a first date and ensure you are properly dressed and groomed before that business meeting. It's also why we rehearse conversations in our heads and practice our presentations.

There's another factor behind first impressions, and that is the concept of "thin slicing." There are simply two things we cannot manufacture more of in our lives: *time* and *attention*. Everyone gets the same number of hours in the day and can only pay meaningful attention to one thing at a time (Yes, even the so-called multitaskers.). Because of this, and the fact that in today's world we're constantly bombarded with information begging for our time and attention, we guard both as a precious resource in a way that we did not a couple of generations ago.

Ding! The smartphone goes off because someone liked one of our online posts. Ding! A new email. Ding! Text message. Ding! Your online news alert. And on, and on, and on throughout the day.

The more we apps we have, the more opportunities for information to head our way. There are, of course, the many work emails, calls, phone messages, live chats, projects, kids soccer practices, the 1,000 XM channels, and infinite information online just begging to be accessed. We've now become skeptical—even cynical—when it comes to information online and moved away from trusting it to seeing it as part of the garbage dump of data making its way into our lives each day.

That general attitude has bled over to people, too. In an effort to safeguard our time and attention, we quickly form opinions of others. In a few minutes, at the very most, we determine whether others are worthy of our time and attention. If we can't physically escape the room, we simply do so in our minds. We check out mentally on our partner, date, business meeting, friend, or presentation speaker, thinking about anything we deem a more valuable use of our headspace.

This is exactly why we fight for attention in our personal and professional lives, and there has to be a hook for others to keep listening. Regularly opening up conversations pointing out your disappointment with others, their flaws, and their mistakes? Not the most compelling reason for others to maintain attention. They may already be getting that speech at home or work. Remember that whatever the reason is, you need to give others a 'good' reason to keep watching and listening. This doesn't mean being inauthentic. That would be a betrayal of yourself and builds relationships on a lie. It does mean, however, that you can pay attention to how you are coming across to others in the crucial first few minutes in your interactions with them, whether in your personal or professional life.

If people never forget how you make them feel, then consider what that looks like after the first couple of minutes of your interaction with them. This doesn't mean you shouldn't hold others accountable for their words and deeds, but someone who is repeatedly made to feel ashamed or inadequate isn't likely to come back to the well for another emotional beating. If your interactions regularly produce negative feelings in others, then expect them to avoid you in future.

The nature of our existence lies between our ears. Perception *is* reality. Others interact with you not based on how you'd *like* them to perceive you but how they *choose* to perceive you. People form judgments and opinions about you based on what you say and do; that's just the reality of it. There's no use arguing against how others feel about you. If you want them to perceive you differently, you're going to have to focus on your side of interactions with them.

So, always be true to yourself. While you might adapt in order to meet the needs of your social surroundings, remember that there's a big difference between responding to the environment you find yourself in and being an insincere version of yourself—one that isn't true to your principles, values, and beliefs.

- *Do you try to look beyond surface impressions when viewing others? Do you attempt to dig deeper to learn more about someone's true nature?*
- *Are you sensitive to the fact that first impressions matter and that people often assess you quickly based on brief interactions?*
- *Are you sensitive to "thin-slicing" and try to promptly build others' desire to keep interacting with you?*
- *Are you sensitive to the fact that how you make others feel **will determine how well you connect with them?***

RAPPORT STRENGTHENS WITH EMPATHY

Empathy is a main precondition for strong emotional connection with others. Before you can identify and satisfy others' emotional needs and desires, you've got to understand their perspectives about themselves and others; their feelings, problems, fears, priorities, and dreams. If you can't envision yourself in someone else's place, you aren't able to properly identify with their state of mind.

Our thoughts create emotions. Our emotions drive actions. If you can't imagine how others think and feel, you're not going to be able to demonstrate sincere compassion, care, and concern for them or understand why they behaved the way they did.

Have you lost a close loved one? Been through a relationship breakup? Experienced failure at work? If so, you may be able to identify with others who are going through similar situations. If not, are you willing to envision what those events look like and how you might feel if you were experiencing them?

Try harder.

Mark, Sanborn says in *The Fred Factor* that "the need to be understood is one of the highest human needs, but too often people who know us either don't care or don't make the effort to understand how we really feel."[65] This is the true value of empathy. When others are empathetic toward us, it satisfies our need for genuine understanding over some superficial acknowledgment of how we might be feeling. When others then show interest in our situation, a desire to help solve our problems, and selfless commitment to alleviate our distress, the foundation for emotional connection is built. We begin to see that others can add value to our lives and want to do so for our benefit not just their own purposes. Without empathy, what we get is some sort of quid pro quo or transactional style of interacting—which might satisfy a surface need but not our core human interests.

There's another benefit of an empathetic approach. By trying to place ourselves in another person's shoes—see what they see, think what they think, and feel what they feel—we are more likely to appreciate and value others. This only bodes well for building more respectful, healthy relationships. You might also find an unpolished diamond within someone's heart or mind if you're simply willing to stop and take a look through their eyes instead of yours. I believe this is what W. Clement Stone was alluding to in *Success Through a Positive Mental Attitude* when he said, "*See* another person's abilities, capacities, and viewpoint. You may be overlooking a genius."[66]

There's an undeniable connection between empathy and motivation. When we can genuinely empathize with others, we can see ourselves thinking, feeling, and acting as they do. We feel others' distress, anger, sorrow, excitement, joy, and pride. Those things motivate others to action. By proxy, they motivate us to action too. You're going to make more of an effort to support others in their time of need or help them celebrate successes when you understand how they are thinking and feeling. If it's negative, you will want to help alleviate the pain. If it's positive, you'll be driven to help sustain the good feeling.

Think about a time you leapt to action to support a friend, loved one, or coworker when they expressed a need. I bet your ability to empathize played some role. In business, this personal skill is both very underrated and highly valued. The ability to empathize often underlies exceptional problem-solving, conflict management, and customer service skills.

By taking the position that others, not yourself, are the most interesting people in the conversation, you feed your own curiosity about them. Others' beliefs, values, experiences, fears, ambitions, thoughts, and feelings all become more interesting. We all like it when others show interest in us. It draws us closer to others because we like feeling significant and attended to. The act of empathizing begins to build emotional goodwill and, over time, you become interested in the person who is interested in you. In reciprocating, the foundation for emotional connection and building relationships is laid.

If you're looking to demonstrate empathy, good listening and questioning skills will be important tools for you. Typically underappreciated, listening and questioning help you demonstrate interest in others, a desire to understand them, and basic respect. It is also an indirect form of influence, as we're often drawn to people who are good listeners. It's attractive to know that others are interested in us and what we have to say. In return, we become more interested in people who are interested in us, hence the benefit for building rapport. Good listeners have the opportunity to ask appropriate questions and provide counsel, which is often why listening skills are prized.

We all like having someone in our lives who is good at giving sage advice. That advice is often preceded by a period of listening and questioning. As John Maxwell eloquently says in *How to Influence People*, "A funny thing happens when you don't make a practice of listening to people. They find others who will … practicing good listening skills draws people to you. And if you consistently listen to others, valuing them and what they have to offer, they are likely to develop a strong loyalty to you, even when your authority with them is unofficial or informal."[67]

- *Do you make a sincere effort to understand others' needs and desires? Do you make their need to be heard and understood a priority?*
- *Can you put yourself in others' shoes in order to identify with what they are thinking and feeling?*

- *Do you use good listening and questioning skills to demonstrate empathy?*

EMOTIONAL CONNECTION IS KEY

If you're going to build relationships—real, strong, enduring bonds—you have to connect with people emotionally. For those of you who struggle with the warm and fuzzy aspect of interactions, this does not mean baring your soul every time you talk to someone. However, people are going to *feel* some way about you over time, as you will about them. Most importantly, being around you is going to make others feel something about themselves. It's better that those feelings cause a smile rather than a frown, right?

If you tend to struggle with emotional connection, just start small and let it grow. Find common ground and interests, and share experiences together. It can be something as small as a shared meal or a casual conversation about the weekend. Try a sincere compliment.

John Maxwell, one of the most prolific and masterful writers on leadership, asserted in *Becoming a Person of Influence* that our aim in building relationships and influencing shouldn't be to get people to think more highly of us; it should be to get them to think more highly of themselves.[68] I love the reminder that the core of rock-solid relationships isn't how we feel *about* the other person; it's about how we feel *when we're with* that other person. Does your partner, friend, boss, or coworker make you feel loved, worshipped, special, respected, supported, significant, included, happy, or confident?

Ultimately, how we feel about others is a by-product of how they make us feel about ourselves when we interact with them. How positive and strong are your relationships with those who make you feel insignificant, flawed, unintelligent, disrespected, unloved, or forsaken? Probably not very. Strong relationship-builders focus on *others*, in particular how they create positive emotions for others. When that happens, guess what? Others tend to return your emotional goodwill and make you feel good about yourself too.

Maxwell's quote also relates to a phenomenon called the *Pygmalion effect*. If you have kids, you've probably witnessed the Pygmalion effect to a degree. Have you ever looked your child in the eye and said "You're going to do great!" when they step onto the sports field, go up on stage for their play or music recital, or prepare to take their school exams? In truth, you're not sure how your child is going to do—and they don't know either. But encouraging and showing faith in them boosts their effort, and they try their utmost to prove your belief in them was well-placed.

This phenomenon has been studied in various environments, from education settings to the military, and research has shown that providing encouragement and showing faith in others *actually increases* their subsequent performance. Listen up, managers and coaches, if you want to get more out of your teams. The secret is out. A word of encouragement and show of faith often helps. This, of course, also goes for the rest of us.

> "… there are people in your life who want to be fed—with encouragement, recognition, security, and hope. That process is called nurturing, and it's a need of every human being … The unfortunate truth is that most people are desperate for encouragement. And even if a few people in their lives build them up, you still need to become a nurturer to them because people are influenced by those who make them feel the best about themselves."[69]

It feels good to have someone believe in you, encourage you, and support you. We like those people. Being a cheerleader for others can help create the positive emotional connections you need to build healthy relationships. Emotional connection is based on experience. It's not about relaying information, building credibility, or proving you're an expert. Those things do have their part to play in building relationships, particularly in professional settings, but if you want to supercharge your relationship-building, you have to elicit feeling in others. As I've discussed, it's about creating positive feelings in others about themselves when they're with you as the first priority and, secondly, positive feelings for you.

Others want to know you can add value to their lives somehow, whether it's moving them toward pleasure or away from pain. Be intentional about the emotions you create and you will, with a little forethought, be able to build healthy relationships more quickly. Sustaining those relationships is then about delivering on the promise you've created through such emotion. Deliver on people's emotional needs and desires and strengthen the connection you've built.

- *Do people think more highly of themselves as a result of interacting with you?*
- *Do you demonstrate faith and belief in others through your words and actions?*
- *Do you encourage and support others to help foster positive emotional connections?*

CONFLICT AND DIFFICULT PEOPLE

The wonderful thing about being the special person you are is that you have your own unique thoughts, feelings, experiences, opinions, values, and beliefs. We are all like snowflakes in that respect; no two people on this earth are *exactly* alike. Our diverse range of experiences brings richness to those we touch. However, because of our—and others'—uniqueness, our thoughts, feelings, and opinions will inevitably run into conflict with others' from time to time.

In business, discussion and healthy debate helps create best practices that propel organizations forward. In our personal lives, it's no different. In order to build and sustain healthy relationships, you must constructively address conflict from time to time. Even the strongest relationships occasionally experience disagreement and conflict.

There will be people out there who do not personally gravitate toward you or like you. There will also be those you don't personally like. That's life. You're an adult and, whether you like someone or not, you must learn to interact constructively with them. The world is filled with lonely, uncompromising people who don't know how to work through conflict constructively and isolate themselves because of it. Don't be one of those people, walking this earth alone.

In the workplace there's a basic expectation that you are able to work effectively with others whether or not you personally like them. In life, the same skill will help you better navigate social situations and personal relationships. Learn to manage disagreement and conflict constructively and you will come to respect yourself more while effectively building and sustaining relationships.

So, what happens when conflict is avoided and allowed to fester? The dark corridors of our minds nourish the growth of conflict when you run from it rather than address it. If you've ever been in a situation where you've been in conflict with someone else and become more bitter and angry about it over time after failing to address it directly, you know what I mean. We've all been there. Eventually we lose all perspective on the issue and all we know is that we're really angry about something. We're not sure exactly what it is anymore, and we can't identify what exactly is triggering our emotions to grow stronger. We're blinded by rage or bitterness, or we're playing the victim, and we can't find our way back to a place where we can constructively address the conflict.

Like mushrooms, the conflicts you hide in the shadows only grow. The ability to force issues into the light where they have to be addressed is a key component of successful relationships. The ability to talk through difficult, emotional, or high-stakes issues involving disagreement and conflict in marriages was found to be a critical predictor of the future direction of such relationships:

> After watching dozens of couples, the two scholars predicted relationship outcomes and tracked their research subjects' relationships for the next 10 years. Sure enough, they had predicted nearly 90 percent of the divorces that occurred. Over time, couples who found a way to state their opinions about high-stakes, controversial, and emotional issues honestly and respectfully remained together. Those who didn't, split up.[70]

This research confirms what we already know through hard experience: suppressing conflict never ends well. It only allows conflict to, at best, limit the positive potential of our relationships or, much more commonly, dooms them to failure. The ability to talk through crucial and sensitive subjects, particularly when disagreement and conflict are involved, is a critical life skill you must develop.

Every relationship has bumps in the road—times when they run into conflict and difficulty. Your skills in talking through problems constructively determines whether those relationships move past disagreement. Hiding from conflict only guarantees that relationship problems persist, and likely grow, in a vicious cycle.

Most of us have learned the hard way what it's like to hide from conflict or handle it poorly, just like we've learned from disagreements we worked through well. I'm no different. I'm not a relationship guru without a record of failure. There are quite a few lessons I've learned in my professional role, as well as in my personal life, which might be of some use.

The first is to pick your battles. Now this might seem counter to the point I have just made about addressing conflict rather than hiding from it, but there is an important difference between being forthright and appearing downright contrary. If there's disagreement, is it over an important issue in the relationship? Is it about an issue of values, core beliefs, ethics, or some other subject that is foundational to your relationship? If so, address it. If not, take a moment to think before you move forward. If others and I disagree about some trivial issue that doesn't affect our relationship and doesn't fuel negative feelings, I consider whether it really needs to be discussed. Maybe it does. Maybe it doesn't.

You do not have to address each and every disagreement or difference of opinion in your life. The risk, impact, and probability of the issue negatively affecting your relationships should be considered. If you spent time expressing your opinion on every issue that runs counter to someone else's, that is all you would do all day and you'd drain emotional energy that could be directed more positively elsewhere. Every battle does not need fighting, and an obsessive need to be 'right' all the time is not an endearing quality. Why conduct an emotional siege over a tiny issue that you could simply bypass to move on to a more important pursuit in your life? There's a crucial difference between addressing conflict and seeking it out, and you must learn that difference.

- *How well do you believe you handle conflict?*
- *Do you avoid conflict at all costs, or address it directly when it arises?*
- *Are you comfortable talking through difficult, emotional, or high-stakes issues?*
- *Do you pick your battles, or go looking for conflict?*

EVERYONE HAS GOALS DURING CONFLICT

Conflict is the *perception* of incompatible goals. This is a concept that lives first and foremost in your mind. You *believe* you're at odds with someone else, so you are. Perception is reality, after all. Whether you move past that belief to explore whether you are actually in conflict, and what can be done to resolve it, is up to you. It's more uncomfortable than simply walking away and burying your head in the sand, hoping that the conflict will magically resolve itself. But it never does. Even if it subsides, if underlying feelings are never addressed they will infect your future interactions with others.

The acute discomfort of dealing with a problem here and now is better than living with the chronic disease that ultimately kills many relationships in the end. We've all experienced this at some point in our lives, and the lost time in addressing the problems can never be recovered.

During conflict, people have *positions* (overt, content-related goals) and they have the *interests* that lie beneath them. Too many people focus only on positions without getting to the core of the issue: *why* others have taken up their positions. Identify the *why* and you can begin to truly address the conflict in a way that helps you understand others better and maintain the relationship along the way.

For example, if I said that my goal was to double my salary at work, which was incompatible with my boss's goals, we have identified two conflicting *positions*. These positions are the seemingly incompatible goals. The real questions that help us resolve conflict are: *Why* do I feel that doubling my salary is appropriate or needed? *Why* does my boss have a different position on the issue? The *why* behind my goal could be (1) I have done market research and concluded that doubling my salary brings me in line with what others are paid for similar positions elsewhere; (2) I have found out that the two other people in my same position within the company are being paid twice what I am; (3) I have a gambling or drug problem and need the additional money to fuel my habit; or (4) I'm getting divorced and need the additional income to pay alimony. These reasons are likely to invoke different reactions from the boss, based on their understanding of why I want my salary increase.

The boss's position that they aren't willing to agree on doubling my salary may be based on (1) The need to control expenses and be responsible with the department's budget; (2) Data that indicates I am already being paid competitively compared to the external market for my job; (3) Information that shows I am being paid similarly to my coworkers in the same position; (4) The fact that my performance in the role hasn't been acceptable or doesn't warrant such a significant pay increase; or (5) The risk to the company of losing me and the ease of replacing me at my current pay and performance levels is one the boss is willing to take.

I'm giving you a workplace example here, but the same would apply to any conflict situation. My greater understanding of why the boss can't agree to my salary increase request, just as the boss's greater understanding of why I made the request in the first place, helps resolve the conflict. As most conflicts are fueled by gaps in perception, the inability to empathize with another's point of view, or communication problems, a greater understanding of each other's interests is a positive tool for conflict resolution. And it always comes back to *feelings* in the end.

I may feel I am being mistreated, disrespected, taken advantage of, or undervalued if I believe I'm not being paid fairly compared to the external market or my coworkers. My raise request might be fueled by fear or anxiety if it is related to my divorce and worry about meeting my future financial obligations. If fueled by my gambling or drug addiction, my feelings could also be fear, anxiety, stress, and the insatiable need to satisfy a destructive habit.

My boss's position to not grant my request may be fueled by their own feelings of fairness, obligation to be a good steward for the company, sense of duty, or fear of repercussions if they did grant the request. We are all human; all emotional beings. Whether in our personal relationships or in the workplace, the fact that our behavior is caused by our thoughts and emotions is undeniable. When you dig deeper beneath someone's position in a conflict to uncover the feelings behind it, you'll make better progress toward resolving it.

In addition to the content goals people have during conflict, there are also *relational* goals. These goals reflect how both you and others want to be treated as you discuss and resolve conflicts. There are some basic premises around relational goals, which include being treated with respect and dignity, being heard, and making a good-faith effort to empathize and resolve disagreement. Avoiding manipulation and coercion are also a part of relational goals during conflict.

When these types of goals are respected by all involved, you create a better atmosphere for resolving conflict. This allows for greater focus on positions and interests without unhealthy distraction. When everyone feels they're being treated with basic respect and that an effort to maintain relationships is being made, then all can get to work on the business of resolving the conflict itself.

Procedural goals during conflict consider what process is being used to create solutions and how decisions on conflict resolution are made. For instance, if three options for resolution are presented to you by the other party instead of you discussing and mutually coming up with potential solutions, you may feel that the process of generating solutions hasn't been fair or inclusive. Likewise, if you don't agree on the process of choosing a solution and feel like you haven't been able to participate or that it was arbitrary or biased, you will see it as unfair and are less likely to respect the outcome.

When we feel like the process is fundamentally fair and rational—and that we've had an opportunity to be heard and our viewpoints considered—even if we disagree with the outcome we're much more likely to respect and abide by it. Bear in mind that when you're in conflict and manipulation and coercion enter into the fray, procedural fairness is sacrificed and anger can run deep.

If you're in a dominant position during conflict, avoid the temptation to impose your will on others for its own sake and be directive. People in weaker positions who see themselves as the victim of coercion and manipulation commonly try to "get even" when the opportunity arises for them in the future. If you choose these tactics, be prepared to get stabbed in the back at some point. It's often terminal for your relationships with others too.

In contrast, when others know you're in a dominant position and could impose your will on them but instead choose good-faith efforts to resolve conflict on equal footing, they'll have greater respect for you and for the outcome—even if it isn't what they hoped for. Justin Bariso, in his excellent book *EQ Applied*, talks about this issue:

> Instead of attempting to exercise dominance, focus on learning more about the other person's viewpoint, as well as the reasons behind their feelings. Then, focus on re-establishing common ground, with the goal of laying a foundation you can build upon later. Above all, strive to leave the conversation on a positive note ... Remember that lasting influence takes time. Your goal isn't to "win the argument" or change someone's mind in a single discussion. Rather, strive to see the bigger picture.[71]

The last goal people have during conflict situations is related to their sense of *self-esteem*. No one likes walking away from conflict with wounded pride and damaged self-esteem. We rarely forget when we lose face and are made to feel insignificant as a result of conflict. When pride is damaged and we feel we've lost our standing, our efforts can unhealthily turn to dragging others down with us. We may also obsessively focus on how to repair our damaged self-esteem, rather than putting the conflict situation in the past and moving forward with the best of intentions. Such damage causes the past to lurk over our shoulder as a distraction until the healing is complete—if it ever is—and inhibits us from looking toward tomorrow.

* * *

- *Do you dig beneath others' positions during conflict to uncover their interests, exploring the "why" behind their goals?*
- *Are you sensitive to how others want to be treated during a conflict discussion?*
- *Do you consider the process of resolving the conflict, ensuring that it's inclusive and considered fundamentally fair to everyone?*
- *Do you help others maintain or enhance their self-esteem during conflict, or do you wound them?*
- *Do you use your dominant power position to force conflict solutions on others, or try to deal with them as an equal partner?*

* * *

CONSTRUCTIVE CONFLICT COMMUNICATION

Remember that *every* conflict of substance is fueled by emotion, which can be deep-seated. If you're dismissive of others' thoughts and feelings, particularly in conflict situations, eventually people stop engaging in conflict with you because it's a waste of their time. When you fail to offer significance and validation to others by at least acknowledging their thoughts and feelings, you force them to find a sense of significance and value elsewhere.

The first principle is *don't get personal*. This often dooms constructive conflict management. When your significant other calls you lazy, arrogant, unfeeling, useless, or impossible, the conflict moves from being about behavior to being a problem about *you*. There's now a flaw with *you*—*your* personality, *your* character, *your* being. The problem moves from what you have done (or not done) to *who you are*. This unfortunate turn in the conversation supercharges conflict.

"You're such a jerk!"

"You're an unbelievable donkey!"

"You're a useless waste of space who is impossible to get along with!"

These kinds of statements make conflict very personal and cause some extreme emotional reactions that only pour gasoline on the conflict fire. When you attack someone's sense of being, damage their self-esteem, and make them feel insignificant, you're going to damage the very foundation of your relationship with them. It may not be repairable after that, so avoid these kinds of missteps and talk about people's *behavior* and how it makes you feel rather than resorting to personal attacks.

Another basic premise of conflict resolution is to *assume benign intent*. That means you should assume that the other person isn't purposely being malicious or intentionally harmful to you until proven otherwise. Most conflicts start with two well-meaning people who simply have different positions on an issue. Don't assume from the outset that the other person has deliberately 'bad' intentions for you or the outcome. If you do, that perception will color all your conflict interactions and almost certainly fuel, rather than help resolve, the conflict. Demonizing others causes your approach to become immediately adversarial, and you'll become an even bigger part of the conflict problem rather than part of the solution.

MAKE IT SAFE, AND AVOID GIVING DIRECTIVES

If you're going to have a useful conversation to explore conflict and resolve problems, you've got to make it safe. This means setting some ground rules. You might set these rules in your mind and choose to respond to others in a way that encourages a safe atmosphere of rational, respectful conversation. It may also need to be done overtly, where you talk through the ground rules for the conflict discussion to come. In either case, remember that people who feel threatened are either going to lurch forward toward a verbal attack (unfortunately, in rare cases, verbal attacks turn to physical ones, which should **never** happen) or shut down and run away. Neither of these situations helps resolve the problem between you.

Be mindful of your own triggers too. I mentioned this in the section about emotional intelligence. Your increased self-awareness will help you control your emotions during conflict. With self-awareness, you can acknowledge when you're beginning to feel unsafe and know how you typically react in such instances so that you don't fall into the trap of *fight or flight*. The hardest, most admirable thing that people do during conflict is to be fully present and have a rational conversation.

Sometimes you have to make an effort to reestablish safety when it begins to crumble. The wonderful book *Crucial Conversations* talks through this subject and supporting techniques like *contrasting* and *finding mutual purpose*.[72] Learning to create a safe environment for discussion is important since we all engage in risky, high-stakes discussions from time to time.

When we sense that either others or ourselves are feeling unsafe, we can step out of the discussion to try to rebuild a sense of safety so the conversation can continue. This can be done by *contrasting*, which is stating what we intend to happen (and what we don't) during the discussion, e.g., "My intent isn't to make you upset or feel inadequate in any way; it is to work through this situation respectfully and come up with a solution that suits us both."

Finding mutual purpose goes a step further to explain how your purposes in resolving a situation are actually aligned rather than in conflict. For instance, a statement of mutual purpose with one of your children might sound like: "You said that you want to move out and become more independent so that you can feel you're truly becoming an adult. I want to see you blossom into an adult so you feel you can stand on your own two feet. In order to make that happen, though, we have to talk through how you are budgeting and spending your money."

There are times, too, when you just have to come right out and reiterate your benign intent for others—that you don't wish them any harm, aren't trying to manipulate them, and intend to make a good-faith effort to resolve a problem in a way that can work for you both. When people don't have to worry about your intent, they can focus on coming up with solutions rather than looking over their shoulders.

If you violate the premise of safety during the conversation and talk or act in a disrespectful manner, apologize. Nothing signals a genuine commitment to work through conflict more than a person who is humble and sensitive enough to hold up their hand and say "I'm sorry" when they've behaved badly or unintentionally injured others. Think about it. When you've been offended by a situation (e.g., problems and mistakes with customer service or products you've bought), you're often unable to move past the anger and indignity until you hear an apology. This doesn't mean that the customer service advisors are admitting fault when they say, "I'm so sorry you're upset and this has happened to you." In fact, you may have actually been the one who caused the problem. What they're attempting to do is acknowledge your discomfort and act with empathy through an apology. You can then move past your own feelings to discuss resolving the actual problem at hand. An apology works the exact same way in personal situations. Once we acknowledge that someone else has been offended by our behavior or injured through our unintentional mistake, we can hopefully then get back to the business of resolving the issue itself.

Avoid giving directives during conflict discussions, i.e., signaling "It's my way or the highway." When you give an ultimatum, you've reduced all of the possibilities for conflict resolution down to only one choice—yours—and created an adversarial environment in the process. You've taken away choice and inclusion in the idea-generating phase of conflict resolution. In stripping someone else of that power, you're likely to offend them and make them feel insignificant. Don't do that.

There's another reason for avoiding ultimatums. Have you ever blurted out an ultimatum during a conflict situation, only to back away from it and reach some compromise with the other person? It happens regularly, and when it does, who loses face? You do. Don't damage your own self-esteem and credibility by careening toward an ultimatum only to back down.

I'm not advocating sticking to your ultimatum once you've given one, which is something people stubbornly do for the sake of pride. I'm suggesting that you avoid that situation in the first place by working with others to come up with solution ideas and settle on one that works for everyone. In this way, you gain credibility as a thoughtful, emotionally intelligent person who can rationally work through problems.

* * *

- *Do you make things personal during conflict conversations, making demeaning comments about others' personalities or characteristics?*
- *Do you try to separate the people from the problem and focus on behavior when resolving conflict?*
- *Do you assume benign intent—that others are well-meaning and don't deliberately set out to manipulate or harm you until proven otherwise?*
- *Do you try to establish a safe environment in which to talk through conflict, using concepts like contrasting and finding mutual purpose?*

* * *

SO, WHAT'S THE *REAL* PROBLEM HERE?

It's important to understand the nature of conflict. Our basic human instinct during conflict is to see others as adversaries. We don't think about the problem as separate from the people. Indeed, the problem is personified by the individual sitting across the table from us—the one who has an opposing view; the person who is making life 'difficult' for us. It's much easier to attach a face to a problem than to view it as something intangible. It seems easier to fight—or run away from—someone than something. For us, the devil always has a face. If we're to manage and resolve conflict more quickly and effectively, we have to peel the mask off conflict and learn to separate people from the problem.

Remember, the problem is a seemingly incompatible view on an issue, or incompatible goals. An issue isn't a person, and neither is a goal. Stop looking at the person across the table as if they have horns and a forked tail and focus on resolving the *real* problem. The first barrier to problem resolution is that each of you see each other as the problem. Flip the script and work to ensure you both are on the same side, *working together against the problem.*

For example, I've worked around debt collectors previously. When a collector calls someone in the early evening to collect a debt, what is the problem in the eyes of the consumer at home? The collector is the problem, of course. The consumer is eating dinner, watching a movie, or talking with the kids, and the collector has interrupted their life to squeeze money out of them. Any experienced collector knows this.

So, what does the collector do in order flip the script and get the person at home to talk to them so they can get the debt settled? They refocus the consumer on the *real* problem and let them know they're working as an advocate to help them against this troublesome issue (the debt). The collector tries to let the person at home know they are on the same side and proposes that if they can only work together cooperatively, they can join forces to successfully overcome the problem.

It sounds easy in theory, but how is it done in practice? Start with using joining language like "you and I," "together," "we," "collaborate," "finding solutions together," "working as a resource to help you," and "join up to solve the problem." These are just examples of phrases intentionally used to subtly and quickly change the atmosphere from one that is adversarial to one of collaboration. These types of phrases also indicate to others that you aren't trying to work against them and that you will take their interests into account when coming up with solutions. If the other person still doesn't understand, you can go a step further by overtly saying, "I'll commit to take both our interests to heart when we try to come up with solutions together."

Remember to use questioning and listening skills to uncover the *interests* beneath the other person's *goals*, or the underlying beliefs behind someone's opinion. Asking "Why do you feel that way?" isn't meant to challenge someone's beliefs and make them defensive; it's meant to better understand them. Everyone wants to be heard. Having a voice is about feeling significant, so don't belittle someone by failing to allow them a platform to be heard. Don't be dismissive of their thoughts and ideas.

The most people adept at conflict resolution get everything out into the open so it can be considered and discussed. "When it comes to risky, controversial, and emotional conversations, skilled people find a way to get all relevant information (from themselves and others) out into the open. That's it. At the core of every successful conversation lies the free flow of relevant information."[73]

Once you both have a better understanding of each other's points of view, begin to generate options for resolution. Make it an open, idea-sharing process where everyone feels it's safe to brainstorm and knows all ideas will be considered. Once you have a few options, discuss the merits and concerns surrounding each and narrow the field to a solution everyone wants to explore further.

Remember that the initial line-in-the-sand ultimatums you might experience are driven by pride and face-saving efforts, and that those positions normally soften when you use the approaches above. Allow others to gracefully back away from their ultimatums if needed. If you can help others enhance their self-esteem—or at least save face—during a conflict discussion, you often achieve a breakthrough that will allow the problem to be resolved. Many people will stubbornly stick to their position simply to avoid a blow to their pride and a loss of face. If you overcome those challenges, a major barrier to resolving conflict is out of the way.

Let's go back to the example of the collector call and the consumer who has a debt of some sort. The collector might say, "No doubt, you're well-meaning and I'm sure would have followed through on your payment commitment if at all possible, so there must have been some challenge that you've run across recently that's made it difficult for you. It's happened to all of us at some point. Tell me more about that so I can help."

The collector has just helped the consumer save face by acknowledging that they are a well-meaning, good person who has run across some financial problem (as have we all) that prevented them from making a timely payment. While later in the conversation the collector will ultimately relay that the consumer is still accountable for taking care of the issue, they will also continue to offer help and ideas to come up with a mutually suitable solution. There's a solution to every problem, after all.

While this might be a rather generic example of a business-related conflict conversation, it works no matter the circumstance. No one likes having their pride wounded, their self-esteem damaged, or their character called into question. When you help others maintain these as one of your conflict-resolution aims, you'll go a long way toward successfully resolving the core problem.

Do you try to join with people against the problem, collaborating with them to resolve the conflict issue together?

Do you avoid giving ultimatums in order to keep options open for conflict resolution?

Do you generate ideas for conflict resolution cooperatively with others, discussing which of them works in both your interests effectively?

NOT EVERY RELATIONSHIP IS WORTH MAINTAINING

Every adult has some relationships that need to be constructively maintained, not because we overtly choose them but because our circumstances (e.g., our jobs or involvement in in some team activity outside of work) require us to make an effort to build and maintain relationships. Now, this isn't to say *at all* that we're driven by fate or circumstance in our relationships. We always get to choose what job, or social interests, we have and those in turn affect who we surround ourselves with.

In all other facets of our lives we get to choose whether to build and maintain relationships with others, and what the health of those relationships looks like (yes, even relatives who you are stuck with by blood). While the human needs for belonging and companionship run deep, relationships shouldn't be collected like trinkets. Relationships should not be about quantity; they should be about quality. Ten mediocre relationships don't equal five good ones. The math of relationships doesn't work that way. And since your time and attention are two precious resources, think about how those resources are used or conserved when it comes to relationships.

Most of us cast a wide net with relationships, particularly when we're younger. The need to be liked, to belong, to feel normal, or to be seen as special in someone else's eyes is a big driver. It can be nice to feel this way, so it's natural that we look for lots of options early on. Other drivers like ambition might cause us to build and maintain relationships as a means to some other end (e.g., career, wealth). And sometimes we try to force relationships with people we know or come to know aren't going to be very suitable partners to fulfill some or all of the above emotional needs. These can be people who just don't resonate with us, whose values and beliefs are fundamentally different than ours, or whose behavior and actions don't align with who we are or want to be. Yet, we forge ahead with our efforts, hoping that some good will come of it.

Please don't misunderstand me. There's good in everyone if we take the time to look. But if we have a choice in how we spend our time and attention, don't we want to use them to build the relationships that are more likely to be fulfilling or that we believe are important? It's a commonly held belief that no one on their deathbed says, "I wish I'd spent more time at work." or "I wish I'd made more money." Regrets typically surround how, and with who, past relationships unfolded. You can write a story that avoids bitterness and regret. You're the author of your own life, so ensure the cast of characters makes it one of happiness and fulfillment if you can. Be intentional about how, and with whom, you spend your time and attention. It's all you've got. You can't buy more of it.

There also might be current relationships that have grown toxic. I mentioned earlier that every long-term relationship goes through difficulties at some point, and your efforts to work through them can also be important for your happiness. There's an inflection point with relationships though—and only you know where it lies—that determines whether you are in or out. If the relationship is worth repairing, try to work through the difficulties. But if you've tried and things still aren't working, or the difficulties are creating a perpetually toxic environment that is unhealthy for you both, then what may seem like the hard decision will likely be best for all involved. End it and move on.

In this case, it's addition by subtraction in your relationships. You're freeing up your time, attention, and emotional energy to enhance the quality of your remaining relationships or enter a new relationship that is more rewarding. You can rid yourself of the dark cloud of unhealthy, unfulfilling relationships. Ask anyone who has freed themselves from a toxic or abusive relationship and they'll likely describe feelings of liberation and renewal from doing so.

If we made a true and full effort with an important relationship and it didn't work out—or we determined that an unhealthy relationship wasn't important in our lives—does it count as a failed relationship? I don't think so, and I don't believe that you should spend time absorbed in guilt or regret either. There are eight billion people out there. Do you really think you can hit it off with them all?

I understand that human needs for belonging and love lead us to look for them in unhealthy places from time to time. Some will even persist in a cycle of abuse rather than feel alone. But remember how special you are. You deserve to feel happy and fulfilled. If your relationship is working against that and you've either made a good-faith effort to repair it or determined that the relationship isn't important for you anymore, why would you persist? If you know what makes you happy and fulfilled, seek and maintain relationships that help with that. If you don't know yet, seek and maintain relationships that you *feel* are likely to help you along the way.

So, if someone is poisoning your well of happiness, drop them and move forward.

- *Do you cling to unhealthy or abusive relationships rather than letting them go?*
- *Are you able to view the ending of relationships as something other than a personal failure?*
- *Are negative or unhealthy relationships standing between you and personal fulfillment and happiness?*

Section Five
SELF-DEVELOPMENT

The need to experience progress and growth is one of the most basic and visceral of human desires. The feeling that we are somehow standing still, stagnant while the world passes us by, can poison our outlook on life. It makes us believe we're shrinking in significance and that the meaning of our existence has somehow been lost. It's the feeling that if we're not learning, we're dying.

I'm a big proponent of lifelong learning. I don't believe there's another alternative, really. I suppose you can choose to remain closed-minded and refuse to apply new knowledge, but that knowledge always occupies that space between your ears somewhere. Ignorance must be exhausting. The emotional energy it takes to steel yourself against the tide of information, like a dam holding back a relentless flow of water, has to take its toll on those who choose pride and ego—or stubbornness and ignorance—over growth and enlightenment.

There are those who ascribe to the belief that some people are just born leaders or naturally talented. They believe in nature versus nurture. I think that viewpoint is just their ego's self-preservation mechanism kicking in so they can believe they're part of some special group. Michael Jordan is quoted as saying,

"I've always believed that if you put in the work, the results will come" and "The more you sweat in practice the less you bleed in battle." Famous soccer athlete Pelé said that "Everything is practice." Legendary cellist Pablo Casals was asked at aged ninety why he continued to practice and he said, "Because I think I am making progress."

These quotes are not from people who believed they were naturally gifted or special, trusting that some innate ability would help them carry the day in their fields. Already at the top of their professions and arguably the greatest in history, something deeper drove them to hone their crafts even further. Learning and growth drove them forward, along with the relentless pursuit of perfection— even if it's a destination that can never be reached.

I'm a big Peter Crone fan and greatly enjoy his views on how the human mind works. I saw a video once in which Peter explained that he hoped he never reached his full potential, because that would mean he would have nowhere else to go in terms of fulfilling needs for personal growth. I think he's exactly right—and that it's impossible to fully realize your potential in the first place. How depressing it would be to have nothing left to learn or improve upon in your life!

The myth about highly talented people must be cast aside. Many talented people got to where they are because of hard work, even if blessed with certain physical attributes (we all aren't six foot six like Michael Jordan). There are many others blessed with some similar gift who didn't reach the same level. For example, I'm six foot eight and Jordan could likely still beat me one-on one seated in a chair with one eye closed. I should have practiced that jump shot more!

I've both heard and said that something special happens when passion and talent collide. We all know that everyone benefits from learning and practice, even those who already operate at a high level in whatever interest or profession they pursue. Again, there is a deep-seated need to feel that we are moving forward down a path rather than standing still. Everyone experiences this desire. Whether learning more about the background, emotional needs, and interests of our significant other or expanding our knowledge in support of our professional growth, something drives us to seek knowledge. Learning is far more fun than ignorance!

A LEARNER'S PERSPECTIVE

If you're going to learn, you need to get your head straight. You need to take on the perspective of a learner. Learners are students, not masters. This means you've got to keep an open mind and accept that you don't know all there is to know about a particular subject—and you never will. If you come to the table thinking "I should be the one teaching this class" or "I know this already" then you're going to terminally distract yourself from a real learning experience. Humble yourself.

Whether within or outside the workplace, pride and ego serve to keep us in the dark by telling us we're already the smartest one in the room, we have no need to learn further, and no one else could possibly have wise counsel for us. As Ryan Holiday states in his truly excellent book *Ego is the Enemy*, "The second we let the ego tell us we have *graduated,* learning grinds to a halt ... An amateur is defensive. The professional finds learning (and even, occasionally, being shown up) to be enjoyable; they like being challenged and humbled, and engage in education as an ongoing and endless process."[74] If you're going to come with pride and ego overflowing from your pockets, you're not going to be able to bend the knee at the alter of learning. Get over yourself and you'll accelerate your pace of growth.

A true learner's humility leads them to value others precisely because they don't believe they already know it all or that others have little to add to their expertise. We're all incredibly special people in some unique way. Just like our fingerprints and DNA are ours and ours alone, so is our unique mix of skills, experiences, values, beliefs, and background that no one else has. In that, surely, we can be a source of learning for others—and others for us.

John Maxwell, in *Talent is Never Enough*, states, "Teachable people are always open to new ideas and are willing to learn from anyone who has something to offer. American journalist Sydney J. Harris wrote 'A winner knows how much he still has to learn, even when he is considered an expert by others. A loser wants to be considered an expert by others before he has learned enough to know how little he knows.'"[75]

We've likely all been surprised by the hidden talents or passions we've discovered in others at some point—the work colleague who moonlights as a wedding singer, the neighbor who is involved in a local community cause, or the friend who built his own house literally from the ground up. Randy Pausch, in his moving lessons for life entitled *The Last Lecture*, said that there is good in everyone; sometimes it just takes a while to reveal itself. I believe the same about knowledge. There's expertise in all of us—something we can teach others—but only if they're open to learning.

So, are you a humble and open-minded learner?

There's an unmasking that humble learning requires. It makes you look in the mirror and admit your shortcomings, frailties, and ignorance in order to purge the pride, ego, and stubbornness that inhibits seeking truth. If you're unwilling or unable to challenge your beliefs and explore the limitations of your knowledge, you'll only serve to widen the gap between who you are today and who you could be on the other side of learning experiences.

> Truth is the first principle of personal development. We primarily grow as human beings by discovering new truths about ourselves and our reality. You'll certainly learn some important lessons no matter how you live, but you can accelerate your growth tremendously by consciously seeking truth and deliberately turning away from falsehood and denial. Genuine personal growth is honest growth. You can't take short-cuts through the land of make-believe. Your first commitment must be to discover and accept new truths, no matter how difficult or unpleasant the consequences may be. You can't solve problems if you don't admit they exist.[76]

- ***Does your ego keep you from learning from others because you believe you already know it all?***

- *Do you believe that each person has unique talent you can learn from?*
- *What hidden talents do you have that others could learn from? Do you know what special talents your closest friends and coworkers have?*

DISCOMFORT, RISK, AND MISTAKES AS PART OF LEARNING

Learning never comes with a guarantee of painlessness or a shield against discomfort. In fact, you likely already know that some of the most valuable life lessons you've learned stung quite a bit. Randy Pausch, in *The Last Lecture*, said, "Experience is what you get when you didn't get what you wanted. And experience is often the most valuable thing you have to offer."[77] Sometimes the experience is painful, but if you're unwilling to step out of your comfort zone to seek knowledge, you're missing out on a massive potential source of wisdom.

If you can admit, as a result of gaining new knowledge, that your assumptions were flawed, your beliefs were wrong, and you've made mistakes, then you're truly learning. If you seek information to only confirm, rather than challenge, your experience and beliefs, you aren't really learning. You're just stroking your own ego.

Learning, innovation, and reinventing yourself aren't risk-free activities. As I mentioned already regarding change, the potential of greater reward often carries inherent risk to your beliefs, pride, and ego. There's a very real possibility you'll make mistakes that will cause both yourself and others pain.

The comfort zone, while shielding you from uneasiness and the pain of mistakes, also inhibits your personal growth and learning. Staying in the comfort zone is failing to step through the door that allows you to explore, learn, and grow. You might get hit by a bus crossing the street or get rained on, but that risk is one you weigh against staying seemingly safe locked in your home all day. The comfort zone is the enemy of leveraging your potential; it's the obstacle blocking your path to greater self-fulfillment.

Environments that don't allow for mistakes—and crucify those who make them—suffocate learning and innovation. This is commonly seen in organizations that use command-and-control, directive management in which staff live in constant fear of losing their jobs and do everything possible to avoid error. There's a great deal of emotional energy burned in constant self-preservation, and that price for work teams is the sharing of ideas and using more of people's experience and potential.

It's no different within or outside of the workplace. In relationships, you may keep your head down, avoid conflict and pain, and decide to play it safe for fear of upsetting a regularly critical significant other, hiding your potential to actively contribute to the relationship and help it blossom. That's also a shame and is likely to doom the relationship in the end.

We improve through learning and, at least in part, through mistakes. This means we must also take responsibility for those mistakes. As Mark Samuel says in *Making Yourself Indispensable*, "Master Learners know that they must learn from mistakes instead of deflecting them, blaming others for them, or hiding from them, which leads right back into the Victim Loop. They have had to develop the courage to change the consequences game from one of punishment to one of learning—every time, no matter what. And if they get punished by others, they still have a default response of learning from the experience rather than giving up in defeat."[78]

Whenever you can, remember that every experience, whether it ends in success or failure, has value. It tells you something. There's a lesson in there somewhere, or valuable information that gets you one step closer to the outcome you hope for. It's wholly unrealistic for you, and anyone who might have a relationship with you, to expect perfection. You will not get it right the first time, or every time, and expecting that blinds you to the valuable lessons that come with mistakes because you are too busy wringing your hands to look for the learning in them.

Remember Thomas Edison's quote on finding 10,000 ways that don't work. Edison held over 1,000 patents and invented the phonograph and the first motion picture camera, as well as many other devices used in electric power generation, sound recording, and mass communications. Imagine where we'd be today if he was less resilient or open to learning through failure and experience.

If you're in an environment, either at work or home, that is totally unforgiving of failure and mistakes, you either need to help others recalibrate their expectations or find a new place to hang your hat. If you don't, you're going to smother your own learning and development and will likely suffer along the way. If your goals involve personal growth, learning, and fulfillment, you can't constantly play it safe or be your own worst critic when mistakes happen.

Perfection, while beautiful, can also be the enemy of learning. When things go swimmingly and everything falls into place, you're unlikely to take the time and effort to reflect and learn from the experience. Perfection can also breed complacency. When mistakes and failures occur, you more often pause and take the time for necessary self-reflection to find the lesson. That's a good thing for your long-term personal development, so give yourself a break when you find out you're human after all.

To find those valuable lessons and supercharge your knowledge gain when mistakes occur, consider these questions that Peter Hollins outlines in *The Science of Rapid Skill Acquisition*:

1. What was the cause of the mistake?
2. Did you make a mistake in the strategy or the method that you chose to follow?
3. Did you make a mistake in execution?
4. What should you have done differently?
5. Were there any warning signs you missed?
6. Did you make any assumptions that turned out to be wrong?
7. Did the mistake reveal any blind spots or skills which require additional practice?
8. Did this mistake reveal a character trait that is holding you back (e.g., pride, inflexibility)?
9. How will you do things differently to avoid the mistake in future?
10. If you saw someone else making a similar mistake, how would you advise them?[79]

To learn from experience—really capture the lesson— you've got to take the time to reflect on what happened, and why, when things don't go as planned (and reflect even when they do). These ten questions are a great tool to help draw learning from mistakes and failure, which are often full of information that can boost our personal growth.

When relationships falter, performances don't go as you'd hoped, and you experience failure, reflecting (not ruminating) on the circumstances that led to the current state well help get you further, faster in life. Why? Because *wisdom = knowledge + reflection*. Elizabeth Day's insightful books *Failosophy* and *How to Fail* are also great resources. They teach us that failure shouldn't be feared, but instead embraced if we're to acknowledge our own humanity and really learn about ourselves and grow.

I'll leave this subject with a parable I ran across about a bear, a wolf, and a fox, likely adopted from *Aesop's Fables*. A bear, a wolf, and a fox were out hunting in the woods and each caught a deer. The bear asked the wolf, "How do you think the spoils should be divided?" The wolf responded, "I think we each should get a deer." The bear ate the wolf. The bear then turned, his mouth dripping with blood, to the fox and asked, "How do you think the spoils should be divided?" The fox responded, "I think you should take all the deer." The bear then asked the fox, "How'd you become so smart?" to which the fox replied, "I learned from the wolf."

Now, your ability to learn may not literally be a matter of life and death, as it was for the fox and wolf, but if you don't learn from your mistakes, you're doomed to repeat them. Part of life's journey is to be able to take what is thrown at us—including the unexpected, the 'bad,' the failures, and the mistakes—and use it to learn and become better versions of ourselves. Don't deny yourself that opportunity by failing to slow down and notice the lessons being taught.

It's important to understand that, while we all like to succeed, it's an extremely rare circumstance for us to gather all the information to make a decision and begin walking the road. We are not omniscient, and information is often hidden in hard-to-reach places. If you wait until every piece of information available comes to you in an effort to manage risk of failure away completely, you'll never get off the couch to take that first step. You'll incite paralysis by analysis when you do lots of thinking but take no action.

So, many of life's lessons are learned only when you're in the game rather than standing on the sidelines observing. Learning—and life—are participation endeavors. Neither are without risk, but it's a rare thing that we regret the things we've done in life more than those that we haven't. Life's a meal to be eaten. Don't leave it sitting on the plate because you're unsure you'll like the taste of everything.

- *Are you willing to sacrifice the safety of your comfort zone for the chance to learn and accelerate your personal growth?*
- *Does your fear of making mistakes cause you to avoid learning opportunities?*
- *Do you take the time to reflect on mistakes and failure in order to learn their valuable lessons?*

PREPARING YOURSELF TO LEARN

While some learning happens organically through experience and reflection, many of our learning pursuits are more productive with some preparation. Brian Tracy, author of *The Power of Self-Confidence*, says, "Every great human achievement is preceded by an extended period of dedicated, concentrated effort. However, there is little to be gained by digging determinedly, if you're digging in the wrong place."[80] If you're aiming to be intentional about your learning, then set goals in order to orient your efforts and motivate you to accomplish your learning objectives. Setting goals allows you to properly focus your efforts and look for the most appropriate resources in order to help you on your learning journey.

So, set your goals for learning. I'm not going to review the details of SMART (Specific, Measurable, Attainable, Relevant, Time-Bound) goals, as this is a well-known concept around setting objectives. SMART goals can be valuable in any of life's pursuits, and there's ample evidence that just the act of documenting your goals improves the chances they'll be attained. So, however you set goals, the point is to set them. Consider what you will look like on the other side of learning. What new skills or behaviors will you be able to demonstrate? What knowledge will you have gained? What will better performance in your work and life look like? In short, how will you *know* you've accomplished your learning and growth objectives?

The better your objectives are defined and tracked, the less chance that your personal growth will occur by chance. Decide what the new-and-improved you will look like after you've completed a major learning and growth experience and how you'll know you've met the learning aims you set out to accomplish. This isn't to say that every learning experience is planned for and intentional—most in life aren't. But if you've identified opportunities for intentional personal growth, preparing for them makes sense.

Excellence is where passion and talent collide. Indeed, it's passion that drives us to hone our talent further. Look at anyone who has accomplished great feats; they were accomplished because of something beyond mere ambition. There was a strong and relentless drive to achieve borne of passion. Pablo Casals, Pavarotti, Monet, and Banksy wouldn't have reached the heights of their life pursuits if they didn't have true passion for music or art. Do you think Lionel Messi, Tom Brady, Lewis Hamilton, or LeBron James would have accomplished what they did without a sincere, deep-seated love of their respective sports?

Consider what motivates you in any endeavor, including your personal growth journey. If it's external reward (e.g., money, fame, or something else that must be given to you by others), you're likely to be on shakier ground than if your motivations are internal (e.g., the learning journey itself, challenge, obtaining knowledge, personal growth, bettering others' lives, or providing purpose or meaning to your life). Remember that external rewards can be bestowed or withheld and may never come. Internal rewards often come as part of the journey, whether it's work, learning, or any of life's pursuits.

For example, let's say my goal was to climb Mount Everest solely for the feeling of accomplishment once I reached the summit. If I didn't reach it, my pursuit would be a total failure. But what if my goal not only included accomplishment but challenging myself personally, having a new life experience, meeting new people, camaraderie, and experiencing a new culture? Most of those aims would be met whether or not I stood on the summit.

So, always consider your motivators—what drives you to do what you do. You will not only come to know yourself much better, but you'll also be able to make better-informed choices that allow you to spend your precious time and energy on the things you're most passionate about. It's that relentless drive borne from genuine love and interest that will help you overcome setbacks and adversity on the way to success. This includes personal growth and learning.

Remember that Michael Jordan wasn't chosen first in the NBA draft. Tom Brady was the 199th pick. Passion drives seemingly less talented people to great accomplishments where those destined for stardom fail (not that anyone would doubt Brady or Jordan's talents!). Rick and Dick Hoyt didn't complete 1,000 running and triathlon races just because they liked exercise. Kayla Montgomery didn't seek to win three high school cross-country titles in North Carolina just because she liked running. It was passion. Ernest Shackleton didn't ensure he and his crew safely returned from Antarctica just because he enjoyed sailing and long walks. Michelangelo didn't paint the Sistine Chapel just because the ceiling was bare. Hagia Sophia and the Blue Mosque were built in staggeringly quick time for purposes that went far beyond providing a roof and walls to shelter people from the elements; they stir the human spirit. Anyone doubting that should try standing inside them without being deeply moved by the experience. Was the Taj Mahal built to satisfy a sultan's pride? No, it was a product of love. It was passion.

There obviously does not have to be some grand, dramatic reason for your learning and personal growth—or for any of your life's pursuits. Most are the product of more routine needs and desires. Just consider why you want to do the big stuff—those pursuits you believe are really important to your personal growth and fulfillment. Exploring the 'why' behind your efforts might just help you stop sweating the small stuff and find your element. When you do, you can pour more of your energy into pursuing the passions of your life.

So, once you identify what it is you want to learn and why you want to grow, you've got to consider the price you're willing to pay for the prize you want. There's a cost for everything, and you've got to be willing to pay it in order to be successful. This might be the cost of time you would spend sitting on a beach relaxing or engaging in some hobby rather than investing in your personal growth. It might involve time away from loved ones or taking your paid work vacation to attend a class. It might be trading the warm feeling you get from being an expert in your field for an opportunity to step outside your comfort zone and pursue something that will widen your horizons. Your pride and ego may need to take a back seat to humility and illumination for the sake of personal growth. People may need to give you feedback that stings in order to move you forward. There also might be a monetary cost involved with your learning and growth.

Many people quit their personal growth initiatives because they are unprepared to calculate how important a goal is to them and what they are willing to sacrifice to get there. They don't calibrate their expectations, and when obstacles arise they choose to turn back rather than figure out a way around or through them. As you can tell by now, I'm a big fan of Randy Pausch's *The Last Lecture*. Randy had a chance to experience the feeling of being an astronaut (weightlessness) because his passion overcame the obstacles between him and that life goal. Most would have likely quit, but Randy found a creative way to fulfill his dream.

Don't go into any life pursuit, including personal growth and learning, blind to the potential level of commitment and costs involved. You're complicit in your own failures when you simply don't want something bad enough to explore the sacrifice needed in order to get there. Even though circumstances may change that affect your determination, it's better to estimate the price ahead of time so you can steel yourself against the trials of the journey. Just like a car, you're tuning up your psyche for the road ahead.

As you plan for growth and learning in your life, it's wise to consider your personal strengths and areas for improvement. Most people aren't adept at identifying either accurately, so get some external inputs if you can. Your own assessment is at least a starting place though—and your own opinion matters too. As you think about your personal growth journey, what have you learned from past experiences, results, and feedback? What personal qualities are going to be useful for you in this next learning adventure? Have past results not gone your way when you've undertaken personal growth initiatives? If not, why not? How much of that was due to external circumstances? How much was due to either your reaction to those circumstances or your own behavior?

American football coach Lou Holtz, known for his endearing personality and wry sense of humor, once said, "Life is 10 percent what happens to you and 90 percent how you respond to it." When circumstances haven't gone your way, whether on your personal growth journey or elsewhere in life, it's always best to look in the mirror and be honest about your level of direct accountability for the outcome. This can be painful at times, but it increases the chances of your next endeavor being successful.

So, consider yourself honestly, including what your unique strengths and qualities are. There are things about yourself to be proud of, which will serve you well as you learn and grow. You must look for opportunities to leverage these things to increase your chance of success. What are they, and how will you use them? As Brian Tracy puts it:

To follow your heart, you don't necessarily need to make dramatic changes in your life or in your relationships. What you do need to do is to see yourself *honestly*, as you really are, and have the courage to channel your energies and focus your strengths into your areas of greatest potential. When you do this, you will soon realize that you have made one of the best decisions in your life. Each person has great strengths and potentialities, and each person is put on this earth to harness those strengths and apply them to benefitting themselves and mankind.[81]

There are also things about you that might inhibit your learning. Identify those as well and be aware when they start to rear their heads. Putting all of these things down on paper is a start, particularly when your personal growth journey is going to be a significant one in terms of required investment. This will help you as you begin to see others' points of view.

I already talked about the value of feedback for self-awareness, and it's a great resource to help you prepare for personal growth initiatives too. Getting input from others will help keep you grounded. It will give you a well-rounded perspective on your learning strengths and areas of opportunity, as well as some advice about your personal growth. You want to go into any important journey in your life with your eyes wide open so you don't stumble off the path. Taking others' feedback and advice into account will help.

- *Do you prepare for learning journeys by setting goals? How will you measure your learning achievements?*
- *Do you know what motivates your personal growth and learning and how you will use that motivation to overcome obstacles you encounter along the way?*
- *Are you aware of the level of commitment and sacrifice likely needed in order to achieve your learning goals?*
- *Have you considered how your strengths and past experiences will help you on your next learning adventure? What things have inhibited your learning in the past?*
- *Do you take others' feedback into account about your strengths and areas of opportunity before you begin a personal growth journey?*

KNOW YOUR LEARNING PREFERENCES AND RESOURCES

As you plan for your learning, it's important to be aware of how you learn best. We don't often consciously consider this, but our personal growth depends on putting ourselves in the best position we can to learn. In general, most adults learn effectively by doing. Simulation and practice allow us to apply what we've learned, hone it, and commit it to memory through repetition.

Initially, some people take in information best visually. For them, a picture is worth a thousand words, and that is their dominant sense when learning. For others, listening is the key form of learning (This is also a skill we all can continue to practice!). They are auditory learners. For most of us, having interaction during learning—discussion, questioning, and debate—adds to the richness of our learning experience. Lectures without interaction struggle to engage people. Some people are very independent learners, able to seek answers with little help or structure. Others require structure and need to attend learning sessions directly in order to hold themselves accountable. For them, independent or online learning may not work well.

Some people highlight passages in books or write in the margins. Taking notes or otherwise recording information you believe is important can enhance your learning retention, and also acts as a reference tool as you apply knowledge in the future. There's less point in learning something new unless we're going to use it somehow. Otherwise, it's just trivia.

As you undertake planned learning, it's also important to understand what resources are available to help you along the way. These will obviously vary based upon what your personal growth subject and objectives are. Someone may have trod the path you are on already, already learning about the subject or issues you're seeking to know more about. Find out what their journey was like and what resources they used to help them along the way. There's a massive array of information out there. The key is narrowing it down to the resources you believe are relevant and will work for your own learning path.

There are books, seminars, retreats, online courses and information, consultants, therapists, and mentors you can access. There may also be other forms of experience-based learning, including volunteering, interim assignments, job rotation, project work, and lateral career moves, some of which apply more to career learning. Some will require more proactive research to gather and make sense of information, and other resources will do some of this work for you already.

Often a lesson sinks in at a surface level, leading you to enthusiastically dive in further because it resonates with you. For me, some of those areas have been personal growth and fulfillment and leadership development. When you consider experience-based learning (where you learn by doing, immersing yourself in activities in order to grow), there are concepts of *job enrichment, job enlargement,* and *framebreaking* to weigh. These concepts, which might be more familiar in the workplace context, can be applied to any area of experience-based personal growth. As I explain these concepts, think of a job as any task, activity, or initiative you'll experience as a part of your personal growth.

First, *job enrichment* involves you performing a familiar task or role to a higher standard than in the past. You might also take lead responsibility for an activity that you've only participated in previously. When you take end-to-end ownership of an initiative, you can see how activities integrate to result in outcomes. This provides greater meaning through an understanding of how individual task performance contributes to overall success. Analyzing a situation or data and making recommendations for action is also a part of job enrichment. Job enrichment is about you diving deeper into a role, activity, or life pursuit to gain more expertise.

Job enlargement is a different method of experiential learning and development. This is when you take on new skills and operate outside of your area of traditional expertise. The job becomes wider rather than deeper as you take responsibility for an initiative that includes activities you haven't previously experienced. It may be one that requires you to interact with new people, technology, or information. For example, Peace Corps volunteers might dig water wells, provide basic education, help with disaster relief, or build schools and housing.

If, like me, you're not exactly handy around the house but volunteer for a worthy cause such as Habitat for Humanity, you work outside of your traditional areas of expertise and learn more about social issues along the way. More and more people are opting out of traditional beach vacations and instead combining leisure time with opportunities to volunteer for social initiatives at home or abroad, and there are tour operators who purposefully arrange such experiences for travelers.

Lastly, *framebreaking* is a concept cultivated by Dr. Mark Kizilos and explained in his book *Framebreaking Leadership Development*. While Kizilos explains the concept in the context of leadership development, I believe this can be applied to any experienced-based learning to accelerate personal growth. Framebreaking involves combining job enrichment and job enlargement, requiring you to go both deeper into an initiative *and* operate outside of your current areas of expertise. The idea is that by challenging yourself on both fronts, you can learn more and more quickly.[82] It's harder in theory, but with greater risk also comes greater reward—if you're willing to step even further outside of your comfort zone. Brian Tracy summarizes the reasons we challenge ourselves in such ways in *The Power of Self-Confidence*:

> … you will never really be happy or satisfied until you have found a way to apply your unique human capabilities to your life and to your career … This is called the feeling of divine discontent. It is a feeling of uneasiness and dissatisfaction that arises whenever you are not fully challenged by what you are doing. To enjoy high levels of self-confidence and self-esteem, you must be working at the outer edge of your envelope. You must be stretching your capabilities continually. You must have a feeling that you are growing, day by day, with the challenges that your work is putting on you.[83]

Opportunities to lead a project or initiative, whether or not it includes job enrichment, job enlargement, or framebreaking, allow you to hone your coaching, problem resolution, resource coordination, and planning skills. You will carry such skills, practiced and grown, throughout your life. Taking charge of a project and seeing an initiative through from beginning to end can be an invaluable learning experience.

Not every path to personal growth is a direct one. Impatient for tangible progress and payoff, we often discount lateral career moves to broaden our knowledge because they don't involve a step up the ladder in title or pay. Delaying gratification in order to truly deepen your learning and grow meaningfully may be part of the cost of your personal growth. Sometimes it will take a longer, more winding route to build the foundation for sustainable, real personal growth. In the end, only you can decide how much you're going to challenge yourself for the sake of your personal growth, determining how far and how fast you're going to go. That will be important for you to consider as you start any planned learning journey.

- *How do you learn best? Is there one sense (auditory, visual, interactive, hands-on) that you prefer to use most when learning?*
- *Do you prefer structure to your learning experience, or to independently research and experiment?*
- *Have you assessed what learning resources are out there to help you along the way?*
- *Have you considered the part experiential learning will play in your personal growth?*

LEARNING ISN'T A SOLO JOURNEY

When you learn, don't make the mistake of thinking that by isolating yourself and making your personal growth journey alone you're going to somehow take more meaning or value from it. We all need some alone time now and then to reflect on our days and the lessons of our lives, as well as have some quiet, peaceful time to recharge our emotional batteries—but learning is not done in a vacuum. Let your alone time punctuate time you spend with others listening, learning, asking questions, and experiencing lessons by doing.

As you begin planned personal growth, consider others to be a crucial resource. The ability to find a mentor can play a critical part in your development. There are people who have either been where you are going or are adept at helping you navigate the journey. Many successful business leaders emphasize the fact that, at some point in their careers, a mentor played a central role in their professional development.

Career and life coaches or people experienced in the areas in which you are looking to grow are out there, just waiting to help you. You obviously need to choose well. A mentor must be someone who not only has the knowledge but can also guide in the ways that you learn best. They also must be someone you can form a healthy personal connection with. I've talked about the benefits of empathetic, considerate support systems in order to boost your resilience, and learning is no different.

In addition to mentors, there are others who can be important players in your personal growth journey. These might be respected role models, trusted friends, and experts in the areas in which you want to learn more. There are also those who have wide networks and can act as pathfinders for you; they know people who know people and can get you connected with others who might be helpful for your particular learning initiative. It's helpful to actually map out your support network. Once you do, you can better plan and organize who you are going to speak with first and who will likely lead you to others along the way.

When you consider your support network, quality counts. John Maxwell, in *The 15 Invaluable Laws of Growth*, references the research of Harvard social psychologist Dr. David McClelland, who found that your reference group (the people you associate with most frequently) may be the dominant determiner of your success or failure in life.[84] Maxwell goes on to say, "You cannot take the growth journey alone, not if you want to reach your potential. The most significant factor in any person's environment is the people. If you change nothing else in your life for the better than that, you will have increased your chances of success tenfold. So think long and hard about who you're spending the most time with, for wherever they are headed, so are you."[85] This is a valuable reminder to be selective about who you let into your inner circle of influencers, including the networks you use for personal growth.

Listen to the people you do choose to allow into your support network. It would be a useless exercise to let people get close to you only to dismiss their counsel. Feedback is a valuable contributor to your emotional intelligence and self-awareness. It's equally useful for your personal growth and performance in any endeavor. It's important to proactively seek and welcome feedback, especially for the purposes of personal growth, learning, and performance improvement.

Getting several perspectives can help ground you and provide a more holistic picture of your strengths and areas of opportunity as you continue your journey. In business, 360-degree feedback is commonly used to help employees gain a more well-rounded perspective of how their behavior and performance is viewed at work. Similarly, take the time in any major learning pursuit to gain early feedback from a variety of sources if you can. It will help you better focus and accelerate your learning. Some of the feedback will sting a bit, but that's exactly the information you need in order to find and stay on your personal growth route. Seeking feedback and placing yourself in the position of student have great long-term benefits for building expertise, as Ryan Holiday explains in *Ego is the Enemy*:

> The power of being a student is not just that it is an extended period of instruction, it also places the ego and ambition in someone else's hands. There is a sort of ego ceiling imposed—one knows that he is not better than the "master" he apprentices under ... updating your appraisal of your talents in a downward direction is one of the most difficult things to do in life—but it is almost always a component of mastery.[86]

- *Do you know who in your support network for personal growth and learning you can draw upon?*
- *Have you intentionally mapped out the network of people you may contact in order to help your personal growth journey?*
- *Do you use mentors, 360-degree assessments, and feedback to help accelerate your personal growth?*

MAKE THE MOST OF YOUR LEARNING EXPERIENCES

Learning, by nature, requires us to humble ourselves and acknowledge that we aren't experts and don't have all the answers. What do we do when we don't have the answers we seek? We ask questions and listen. Questioning and listening skills are often underrated, particularly in today's world, but they are critical skills to building and maintaining relationships, working through conflict, delivering great customer service, negotiating and persuading, and maximizing our learning.

Good questions are relevant, demonstrate that we've been listening, build on prior information to drill down for detail, and confirm our understanding of a subject. They also help uncover what people are thinking or feeling as they make decisions and take action. They allow us to get inside others' heads and empathize with them.

You can't be a learner without being a listener. Maximize your learning by listening empathetically in an effort to truly *understand* what others are saying, not just hear the words. There's a plague of inattentiveness in today's world, where our minds quickly wander off when others speak and we listen with the intent to respond rather than to understand. We think, "Please hurry up and finish what you're saying *so I can say what I want to say.*" That's not listening; that's killing time between your own speeches.

Remember to make an active effort to empathetically listen, suspending your judgment until someone else has spoken and you've had some time to reflect on their message. Use eye contact to maintain your attention with the speaker if you can. Don't interrupt. Put down that cell phone and stop surfing the internet. Multitasking is the enemy of proper listening. Asking relevant and clarifying questions also signals active listening.

True wisdom is gained only when reflection is a part of the process. As you gain knowledge and undertake new experiences, reflecting on lessons learned and how they help you grow is important. Take time to make sense of it all and understand what it might mean for your life. There's great value in the pause. The pause is where real learning takes place. Imagine what would have happened to the fox, for example, if he failed to pause and learn from the wolf's unfortunate demise. John Maxwell says it most eloquently in *The 15 Invaluable Laws of Growth*, "There's an old joke that experience is a hard teacher because the test is given first and the lesson is given afterward. That's true, but only if the person takes time to reflect after the experience. Otherwise, you receive the test first and the lesson may never come."[87]

Listening, questioning, and reflecting are key skills for personal growth and learning. These things are important not just for the enjoyable, interesting subjects you want to learn but also when hard and unpleasant life experiences occur. We often get so wrapped up in self-recrimination, regret, or other emotions that we fail to take advantage of the lessons hardships teach us. Some of our resilience coping techniques involve reflection and taking meaning from adversity to help ourselves learn so that we can cope with life's next challenge even better. There are lessons everywhere—even in 'bad' times—if we're willing to seek them out.

Make sure you're an active participant in your own learning and personal growth. You own it, after all. You make the most out of the journey when you're actively blazing the trail and not just a passenger. Once you spot the lessons along the way, work to apply them in your life. Remember that we learn best by doing—taking knowledge and applying it in practice to see the effects, then tweaking the process based on the results. Moving from unconsciously unskilled to mastery, where you instinctively perform, takes commitment and practice. And practice, by its very definition, involves application. It's theory in action. So, if you want to learn and grow, get both your mind and your hands moving.

How will you know when you've been successful in your planned personal growth journeys? You'll need to assess where you are somehow, so setting your objectives before you start, including some form of a measurable goal, is wise. You can then determine how successful your learning has been and assess whether you have to continue the journey in order to reach the level of personal growth you were seeking. When you put in a lot of time and effort, calculating the return on that investment is smart.

- *How would you rate your listening and questioning skills today?*
- *Do you multitask while listening, and just listen with the intent to respond? Or do you practice empathetic listening, with the intent to truly understand the speaker?*
- *Do you take time to reflect on your experiences and knowledge gained to truly use them as learning resources?*
- *Do you take charge of your personal growth and learning today, or are you just a passenger in the process?*

WHETHER YOU THINK YOU CAN OR THINK YOU CAN'T, YOU'RE RIGHT!

One of the last things to bear in mind as you undertake personal growth and learning is that you're stronger, better, and more special than you think you are. You're the product of life's wonderful mystery—a boundless, limitless individual who absolutely has the ability to find joy, fulfillment, and greatness in yourself. You might not see it today, and others might not yet have pointed it out to you, so I'm doing so right now. You deserve to prosper and be fulfilled, however you define what that means in your life—and you are also the agent who makes it happen.

Take the advice of Thibault Meurisse about your perspective on your limitations in life. In his book *Success*, he says, "Our vision of life is nothing more than a constructed reality. We weren't born with limitations on what we can or cannot do. Those limitations were artificially created afterwards. What your current mindset and way of thinking identifies as impossible could very well sound perfectly achievable for someone else with more empowering thoughts."[88] American industrialist Henry Ford said it even more simply. He stated, "Whether you think you can or think you can't, you're right." Be right about what you *can* do and your thinking will carry you to the places you want to be.

Section Six
MANAGING OUTCOMES

We've already established what a great person you are and that you should feel good about the successes you've had and challenges you've overcome in order to get to today. There are people out there much better off for having been around you. It might have only been a small act or word of kindness when someone needed it most, but you've made a difference. Feel good about where you are today, even if it isn't where you intended to end up when you charted your course some years back. I want you to be well, find contentment, and experience a life of fulfillment and prosperity. Remember that you deserve it.

Managing outcomes will absolutely help you along your journey. We all like to be 'good' at something. Success feels nice, and competence and a record of achievement boosts our self-esteem and feeling of significance. No one prepares for any work or life challenge by thinking, "I'd really love to do a mediocre job today." While a lack of skill, motivation, or interest in particular activities might contribute to performance problems, no one actually sets out to underperform against their potential. However we define it—whether it's in learning, building relationships, managing conflict and adversity, or achieving in some other realm—success is an ingredient in our recipe for happiness and fulfillment.

Anyone who has experienced repeated failures can identify with the feelings of insignificance, inadequacy, and frustration that accompany them. Doubt about our worth and our place in the world begins to creep in, and we unfairly judge ourselves for *what we produce* rather than *who we are*. We tell ourselves, "I'm such a loser," as if life is a contest or something to be conquered. Life is to be lived, not overcome.

We grow and learn from experience. Struggle and failure are often better teachers than repeated, easy successes. The latter tend to breed complacency and arrogance if we're not careful. Both continual failure and constant success present danger to the human psyche, although it's natural to desire success over failure. But our fulfillment and prosperity—however we define them —are better created with our own two hands than left to the mercy of chance and fate. Hope is not a life strategy, and happy accidents aren't to be counted on. If you're going to take control of your life's direction and navigate your way toward happiness, you'll need to manage the outcomes of both circumstance and your efforts.

UNDERSTAND IT, OWN IT, AND INSPECT WHAT YOU EXPECT OF YOURSELF

If you're going to manage outcomes successfully, the first thing you need to do is understand them. Former United States diplomat Henry Kissinger aptly explained the importance of defining outcomes when he said, "If you don't know where you're going, every road will get you nowhere." This is the reason we seek to understand what others expect of us—and what we expect of ourselves. By defining exactly what the goal is, we know how to better focus our efforts and what success will look like once we've achieved it.

Have you ever worked for a boss who wasn't clear about what he or she expected of you and, as a result, you wasted time and effort doing things that didn't contribute to the (undefined) goal? The boss might then have given you a less-than-stellar performance appraisal or chastised you for doing the 'wrong' things even though the 'right' things were never outlined. Frustrating, wasn't it?

You both own the results in such cases. The boss has an obligation to be clear when forming and communicating expectations, as one of the primary duties of leadership is to manage performance through the efforts of others. You have an obligation too, though. In the absence of clarity about expectations, you need to ask questions and confirm your understanding of the goals and how they are measured. Don't allow yourself to be a passenger in the process when you should be taking an active role in successfully managing outcomes.

The example about outcomes in the workplace is an obvious one but managing outcomes in any facet of your life works the same. It starts with understanding what outcomes you desire (i.e., defining the goals). In *The 85% Solution*, Linda Galindo says, "Defining *success* is the best way to get some focus in your life. It's a personal statement about the future you want—as of now. It's a brief, to-the-point outline of what it means to you to be successful."[89] Studies have shown that just the act of writing down goals increases their chances of being attained. And well-formed goals (SMART goals) will further help your understanding so you can effectively focus your efforts and resources. If successful execution is rooted in clarity, and clarity is borne from simplicity, then make your goals as simple and easy to understand as possible. When you close your eyes, can you clearly see what a successful outcome looks like? Does it feel real and appear vivid in your mind's eye?

You are both the boss and the laborer in your own life, so you can improve your relationship with yourself by defining your expectations, committing them to record, and confirming your understanding of your own goals. If you struggle with this, you need to go back and work on your expectations until they evidence the value of simplicity. A good litmus test is to hand your written goal to someone else and ask them to tell you their understanding of it.

Using measurables adds a layer of support for expectations. Measurables (also known as metrics or Key Performance Indicators) will help you assess your degree of success in achieving your aims. They're a tool to hold you accountable for your results. If you said that your goal was to continue your education by taking some college courses and that you would just do your best, those aren't well-defined objectives or supporting measurables.

However, if you said that your goal was to continue your education by completing a Master's Degree in Finance you'd have a more well-defined objective. If you also stated that your aim was to complete the degree within the next thirty-six months and achieve an overall GPA of 3.0 or higher upon graduation, you'd have two supporting measurables to help assess your level of success: (1) Did you achieve the degree? (overall goal); (2) Did you do so in the timeline you set? (timeliness); and (3) did you achieve the GPA you aimed for? (work quality).

Good measurables keep you accountable for achieving your goals since they aren't fuzzy and can't be rationalized as being met. If you simply said, "I took some college courses and tried my best," that is unlikely to get you as far or as fast as defining your objectives—and the metrics that support them—in a clear and precise way. Well-formed expectations and supporting KPIs force you to up your performance game, and if you're serious about achieving a goal in support of your personal growth and fulfillment, you'll use these tools well. Techniques commonly used in the workplace to support performance also apply to any area of your life where you want to manage outcomes.

I've talked about accountability at length already, and accountability is absolutely an important ingredient in managing outcomes. Without a feeling of personal responsibility and obligation related to performance, it falters—or at the very least is less than it could have been. If you're not in the workplace and don't have someone else periodically looking in on you, how do you remain accountable? Remember that you are *always* accountable to yourself.

We've all felt a strong sense of personal accountability at some point, whether or not there's some structure or person to keep us moving toward our performance goal. Our sense of pride in having accomplished our aims, desire for achievement and significance, competitiveness, or feeling of obligation to ourselves and others have all driven our performance in the past.

I mentioned the value of written goals and KPIs. Once something is down on paper, it's there to stare you in the face as a record of what you intend to accomplish *if* you follow through and apply yourself properly.

And if you share those goals with others, you increase your accountability as you now have a network of other people watching and waiting for you to perform. If there are others who are positively impacted by your successful outcomes, envisioning your effect on them is another way of maintaining personal accountability.

Follow-up is another critical aspect of performance management. You've got to inspect what you expect to maintain healthy accountability and control your path to success. When you follow up regularly, you build in opportunities for course correction and can make smaller adjustments before they grow into problems that completely derail you from your path to accomplishment. Think about it like parking an aircraft carrier. If the captain needs to make an adjustment, it's best done as early as possible and while the course correction needed is small. It's *just a little hard* to maneuver a floating city if the parking spot is overshot. So, inspection is a basic aspect of performance management and enables us to be better captains of the ships of our lives.

Set a regular cadence of follow-up for yourself and put it on the calendar. By checking in with yourself to assess your progress and results, you'll be able to make adjustments to your approach. You'll be able to hold yourself accountable and ensure that what you achieved today/this week/this month was more important than anything left unaccomplished. When we know that there's follow-up coming and that we'll be held accountable for our efforts and results, we all tend to up our performance game so that there's a good story to tell. That's one of the main aims of inspection, after all.

Follow-up also helps you coach yourself when results aren't as intended. This is a part of your personal growth and learning journey. Building in regular opportunities for inspection allows you to coach yourself for performance. Adults often learn in the following manner: *act, reflect, adjust, then act again.* Inspection allows us to review and reflect on what is going well and decide what requires a different approach in order to be more successful. We then make the adjustments and act on them and, the next time we inspect, we'll see if outcomes improved as a result. This is continual improvement in action. If you don't follow-up with yourself, you'll miss scheduled opportunities for reflection, coaching, and adjustment that will help you reach your goals.

Also remember the other important functions of follow-up: recognition and reward. When you regularly follow up, you have built-in opportunities to praise yourself for your progress and accomplishments. You learn to become your own cheerleader, and all of us know how good it feels to have someone rooting for us. You need to make sure you're in that cheering crowd yourself. Inspection allows you to recognize how far you've come and feel good about it. Remember that even if you're not quite where you'd hoped to be, you're still drawing breath and are further down the path of your life's journey (even if the path is sometimes unexpected)—and that should feel good to you. Well done.

- *Do you set clear and specific goals for yourself? Do you write them down?*
- *Do you use measurables to help you assess how well you've performed against your goals?*
- *Do you consider why you feel accountable for achieving your specific goals? How will you or others be positively impacted if you perform well?*
- *Do you build in regular follow-up in order to assess results, coach yourself, reflect and make course corrections, and praise yourself for progress?*

TALENT + PASSION = PERFORMANCE

You have access to resources to help you positively manage outcomes. The first of these we've mentioned already, which is your sweet spot. This is where your talents and your passions intersect to allow you full and focused effort on performance. If you know what you have a passion for and what you are 'good' at, when you have opportunities to leverage both, there's a better chance of a positive outcome. Bill George, in *Discover Your True North*, describes your sweet spot as " … the intersection of your motivations and your greatest strengths. When you are operating in your sweet spot, you feel inspired to do great things and confident that you can accomplish them because you are using your strengths. Having an awareness of what motivates you and understanding your strengths and weaknesses enables you to discover your sweet spot."[90]

Self-belief in our ability to manage outcomes successfully comes from a phenomenon called the competence-confidence cycle. We believe we are talented ('good') at something, so our confidence in our ability allows us to dive in and meet the challenge directly. We perform the task successfully, and the positive outcome boosts our confidence and our interest in further honing our expertise. We apply time and attention to building our skills further. The next time a similar task comes along, we are even more confident because we now have a record of success and have developed our talent even more. We dive into the task again, and a positive outcome occurs. We see it, and others see it too. They begin to form positive impressions about our competence (just as we have been doing in our own mind), and their belief in us boosts our confidence another level as we dive into the next task. And on, and on, and on it goes.

If you have talent and passion for certain pursuits, you already have the basis for a high degree of self-efficacy (confidence + determination). That's a solid foundation for good, consistent performance. Wherever you can, leverage your talent and passion to help you be successful. This isn't to say that you should try to tackle only life pursuits for which you have talent and/or passion. As I mentioned earlier when talking about self-development, stepping outside of your comfort zone and areas of expertise is a crucial element of learning and personal growth. You just need to make decisions and balance personal growth and performance from time to time as part of encountering certain situations in your life. Sometimes one has priority over the other.

There's a great benefit to leveraging passion in your life, whether or not you have the talent to accompany it today. As Lee J. Colan states in *Engaging the Hearts and Minds of All Your Employees*, "Performance without passion tends to falter during tough times or in the face of challenges that require sacrifice, significant extra effort, or unusually creative solutions."[91] We don't always have a passion for everything we need to accomplish in life. Those mundane, boring tasks at work and home still need to be done. When you have an opportunity to choose your pursuits, however, just remember that *passion + talent = excellence*. Where one or both elements are missing, you still need to try to manage outcomes effectively, and there are other tools available to help you in those cases.

- *Where do you believe your talents lie today? What are you 'good' at?*
- *What have others told you your strengths are?*
- *What pursuits in life or work are you passionate about?*
- *Do you put yourself in positions to leverage your strengths and passions?*
- *In what area(s) of your life could your talents and your passions intersect? How do you think you would feel applying both of them at once?*

PEOPLE ARE YOUR NUMBER ONE PERFORMANCE MANAGEMENT RESOURCE

Among the tools you have for managing outcomes, the most obvious is the one I've also spoken about previously: your network of people. As with every journey in life, you're only as alone as you want to be because others exist, whether or not they are known to you today, who can act as pathfinders for you when needed. Understanding the nature of your relationship with others as you manage performance can be important for achieving successful outcomes.

If you've never thought about sketching out a *stakeholder map* for important performance activities, you should consider it. This can be done for any area of your life where you are looking at performance, whether it's in your personal life or at work. A stakeholder map is simply a list of people who can affect, or are affected by, your performance. In the workplace, these may be bosses, peers, internal customers, external customers, and others who can act as resources for you. List (1) who they are; (2) the nature of their relationship to you (Do you answer to them for your output? Are they a resource to help you with your performance inputs? Are they affected by the outcome of your efforts?); and (3) how they can provide information to help you manage outcomes.

Everyone has something potentially valuable to give you—and that is often information. This might be in the form of counsel about how your outcomes also affect them, or it may be feedback about your performance and behavior. We've discussed how good feedback can be like nuggets of gold in your life. It can be particularly crucial when you are looking to manage your performance. Seek it out whenever you can.

In addition, everyone has the benefit of some experience or observation in their lives. Others can relay the lessons they've learned to help you clear the fallen trees from your own path. It's been said that if you don't learn from your mistakes, you're doomed to repeat them. I also believe that *if you don't learn from other people's mistakes, you're doomed to repeat them as well.* Where would the fox be today if he hadn't learned from the wolf? He'd have been the bear's next meal.

We all have metaphorical bears waiting to bite us—or worse—if we aren't sensitive to life's lessons. Observe, ask for help and counsel, and seek feedback. Ensuring good flows of communication about your performance and what's affecting it is key to managing outcomes successfully. Because you may be accountable to others, in addition to yourself, for your performance, establishing good flows of communication directly benefits you. This is critical at the beginning of any performance initiative, when others relay their expectations and you gain an understanding of what successful outcomes look like in their eyes.

Producing one, high-quality work item by the deadline when three were expected isn't going to win you any fans. Likewise, producing poor work just to get it done isn't going to gain you the respect of others—including yourself—either. When others are affected by your outcomes, you can only understand expectations by communicating. This includes careful listening and asking questions to clarify your understanding of what others are looking for as outcomes of your efforts.

Ensure there's regular cadence for follow-up discussions so that you can gain coaching and feedback. Whether it's your boss at work or others who critically affect, and are affected by, your efforts in life, touching base regularly will help you establish good flows of performance communication. It also gives you an opportunity to provide your own progress updates and information about where you may need help to positively manage outcomes.

If you're struggling to perform and need help, don't suffer in silence and let your underperformance be an unpleasant surprise. Others can't help you when you are already stumbling in last over the finish line. The time to let them know about your struggles is long before that, when they can provide you help that will actually affect the outcome of your race. When a deadline is missed or you have already finished the task, knowing it isn't the quality intended, then it's already too late to involve others in a meaningful way. You've forced them to become observers in the process rather than providing them an opportunity to share useful input that can help you achieve outcomes that benefit everyone involved.

- *Do you know who is in the network of people that can help you manage outcomes successfully?*
- *Would sketching out a stakeholder map for important performance initiatives help you?*
- *Do you do a good job of leveraging your network of people for help, counsel, and feedback about performance?*
- *When you experience struggles performing, do you hide them or do you promptly inform others and reach out for help?*

OTHER TOOLS FOR MANAGING OUTCOMES

Addressing your time and workload is important for performance management. Time is not a renewable resource—once it's gone, it's gone—and treating it like the precious commodity it is will be critical for your success. This doesn't mean that your entire life should be on a schedule. That would kill the spontaneity in life that makes it fun. However, for big tasks that you do have to manage outcomes for, considering how you use your time is vital to their success and scheduling helps. Periodically reviewing how you did in terms of sticking to the agenda will assist you too, as you'll understand whether you need to alter your behavior to use your time more effectively or the schedule itself needs to be adjusted.

The humble checklist can be another simple tool for managing outcomes. It might seem basic, but the greatest ideas often are. When it comes to things you deem important that need to be addressed, putting pen to paper helps you both remember them and commit to getting them done.

Chip and Dan Heath wrote a fantastic book on managing change called *Switch*. They discuss the value of checklists, stating, "people fear checklists because they see them as dehumanizing—maybe because they associate them with the exhaustive checklists that allow inexperienced teenagers to operate fast-food chains successfully. If they think something is simple enough to be put in a checklist, a monkey can do it. Well, if that's true, grab a pilot checklist and try your luck with a 747."[92] I love this take on the subject. It's a reminder that whether it's the honey-do list of tasks around the house to be completed or a company executive organizing her workload, checklists can be useful for everyone.

Some two hundred years ago, German poet, scientist, and statesman Johann Wolfgang von Goethe said, "the things that matter most should never be at the mercy of the things that matter least." He was speaking about prioritization. If you're going to manage outcomes successfully, you need to understand what things are most crucial and what can wait. The things on your checklists that have strict deadlines and/or are very important to accomplish might be your code-red items. Secondary items might be code yellow for you. Items that are unimportant and you'll get to if you can, or those that have deadlines far in the future, might be your code-green tasks. This system has worked for me in past, but you'll find one of your own that works well for you.

We've mentioned using milestones to eat the elephant one bite at a time by splitting large or long-term goals into more manageable pieces. This is a technique often used in project and change management. When something seems overwhelming or far in the future, there's value in breaking it down. For instance, if there's a major change you're planning in your life, thinking about it in its entirety can overwhelm you and cause stress. That's because you're traveling the entire emotional journey in your mind's eye all at once.

Consider the words of Chinese philosopher Lao Tzu, who said, "A journey of a thousand miles begins with a single step." Don't think about everything that must be done in the next six months to achieve the goal. Worry instead about this week. What tasks need to be accomplished in the next seven days? Or just today? Before you know it, if you've managed each individual day or week well, those weeks string together to get you to your ultimate goal.

Another benefit of using milestones is that it creates urgency. By breaking a long-term goal down into items you've got to take care of this week, you're creating some immediacy for things to get done. Urgency helps hold you accountable for making progress. In addition, when you successfully reach each milestone, you can rightly take a bit of time to admire it and appreciate yourself for the progress you're making in your life. This fuels you emotionally for the next stage in your journey.

Reviewing *risk* and *impact* can also be vital to outcome management. Risk is an element of making decisions. Choosing a path based on minimizing the risk of bad outcomes and maximizing the chances that the outcome will be desirable is common to making decisions. It helps us narrow down choices to those that seem to offer us better overall chances of success.

Mitigating risk is another part of managing outcomes. When we consider the probability of a 'bad' outcome occurring, and the size of the negative impact if it does, we can then decide whether or not to take action to mitigate it. These are actions that, of course, are done to decrease the chances of that 'bad' outcome occurring in the first place, and if it does, to lessen the negative impact. When you try to weigh the probability of an outcome—either 'good' or 'bad'—and the size of its impact (either positive or negative), you help manage risk and reward as well as improve your critical thinking skills.

In managing outcomes, impact can also be thought about in a different way. First, what are the circumstances you *can* impact? Remember, I previously talked about having to adapt to things you cannot change so that you can focus on positively impacting the things you *can* influence. This is outcome management at work. Consider, too, where you can make the most significant positive impact (keep in mind *talent + passion = excellence* as you calculate this) and where you can make immediate impacts.

Lastly, what are the greatest opportunities to do things that don't have a payoff today, but will reap significant rewards further into the future? A little extra pain now, by putting in additional effort or delaying gratification, could provide you a much larger payoff in future. Consider what you are good at and have passion for, where there is low-hanging fruit that can provide you quick wins to build positive momentum, and what decisions are wise long-term strategic decisions. By doing so, you can use the ideas of *risk* and *impact* to positively manage outcomes in your life.

- *Do you use checklists, calendars, and other tools to organize your time and work? Do you prioritize tasks?*
- *Do you use milestones to break down large, complex initiatives you want to get done into bite-sized pieces you can more easily accomplish?*
- *Do you manage risk today in your decision-making? Do you weigh the probability of 'good' and 'bad' outcomes and the impact of those outcomes to decide on courses of action?*
- *Do you consider where you use talent and passion together to make the greatest positive impact in your life and the lives of those around you?*
- *Do you consider where there is low-hanging fruit that allows for quick wins to build your confidence and momentum for success?*

- *Do you delay gratification, sometimes making decisions that require more pain and effort today, for a much greater payoff in the future?*

MANAGING OUTCOMES IS NOT GLAMOROUS

Managing outcomes successfully requires hard work and effort. Of all the tools you possess, none are more potent than your dedication and labor. Your full attention to the task at hand and willingness to see any endeavor through will get you further than any of the other resources you may have. Plenty of talented people have proven themselves unable to navigate their way to success simply because they lacked the work ethic and/or sincere desire to positively manage outcomes. They just didn't want it bad enough. They were unwilling to bridge their desire and a successful outcome through dedication and toil. Success isn't easy. If it were easy, everyone would have it. British chemist and author Douglas H. Everett once said, "There are some people who live in a dream world, and there are some who face reality; and then there are those who turn one into the other." He knew that the ability to forge a better tomorrow, whether for yourself or others, isn't something that everyone is willing to develop and apply. Ryan Holiday, in *Ego is the Enemy*, echoes this sentiment as he relays the story of Edward Degas and his friend Stéphane Mallarmé:

> The painter Edward Degas, though best known for his beautiful Impressionist paintings of dancers, toyed briefly with poetry … One day, Degas complained to his friend, the poet Stéphane Mallarmé, about his trouble writing. "I can't manage to say what I want, and yet I'm full of ideas." Mallarmé's response cuts to the bone. "It's not with ideas, my dear Degas, that one makes verse. It's with words."[93]

Dreaming big is easy; we all can do that. We often aspire to fast-forward to greatness without paying our dues; without experiencing the pain, effort, dedication, adversity, or despair that make triumph so joyful. We feel best about accomplishment when we earn it. Do the everyday things consistently well before you aspire to accomplish big dreams. You'll find that when you do the ordinary things extraordinarily well, you build the foundation for consistent success. Some accomplishments occur because of luck. That's not a sustainable strategy for managing the path of your life. Forge it instead on hard work and effort and you'll find that, together with your talents and passion, you'll be an unshakeable force.

SOME FINAL THOUGHTS

We've now covered a lot of ground together, you and I. From the critical roles of emotional intelligence and building relationships to resilience and managing change and outcomes, there's a lot to think about as you consider your road to fulfillment and prosperity. Life isn't a race to be finished, or a task to be completed, or a trial to be overcome. There's no contest and no winner's medals given out. The wonderful thing is we all define happiness and success in our own way. No one can, or should, tell us what those definitions are. We create them for ourselves using that space between our two ears. Your fate is in your hands, and you have the talent and resources at your disposal to navigate your way to the life you want. Don't give that power away by allowing others to define what joy and prosperity look like for you. Only you can truly know your own heart. No one else is exactly like you, so treat yourself as precious. There will never be another just like you drawing breath on this earth.

Bitterness and regret have a corrosive influence on the soul. Negatively obsessing about your current circumstances does nothing to change them for the better and sacrifices the quality of your current circumstances for the sake of the past. There's a difference between learning from experience and ruminating about it. We've all visited the land of regret; just make sure you don't set up residence there instead of living your life today. I'm reminded of the choices we can all make regarding our attitude toward ourselves and others by a Native American proverb which Diana Whitley relays in *Appreciative Leadership*:

One evening an old Cherokee man told his grandson about a battle that goes on inside people. He said, "My son, there is a battle between two wolves inside us all. One is bad. It is anger, jealousy, sorrow, regret, greed, arrogance, self-pity, guilt, resentment, inferiority, lies, false pride, and superiority. The other is good. It is joy, peace, love, hope, serenity, humility, kindness, benevolence, empathy, generosity, truth, compassion, and faith." The grandson listened and thought for a while. Then he asked his grandfather, "Which wolf wins the battle?" The grandfather smiled and replied, "The one you feed."[94]

Bitterness, anger, and regret take up a lot of emotional energy and can rob you of time and life quality. We've all been there, but as you chart a course to fulfillment and prosperity in your own life, I encourage you to avoid hate's rocky waters. The path to happiness and success in any life never runs through them.

Thank you for exploring this journey with me. I hope, in any small way, you've learned a little more about yourself and some of the abilities you can grow and apply in your own life to lead it well—however you define that. As much as anyone can, I wish you the fulfillment and prosperity you are seeking, and I hope you'll help others get there too.

ABOUT THE AUTHOR

William Schirmer is a senior management professional in Human Resources, having been involved with HR, Talent Management, and Learning & Development functions for domestic and international firms for more than twenty years. His expertise includes the creation and deployment of interpersonal skills training and leadership development programs for a number of organizations. William holds USA, UK, and global Human Resource certifications. His undergraduate study in Political & Behavioral Sciences was completed at Minnesota State University, Mankato in the USA. William completed his graduate degrees in Human Resource Management at Fort Hays

State University in the USA and Social Sciences at the University of Leicester in the United Kingdom. William grew up in Minnesota and is a lover of the outdoors, travel, motorcycling, and exercise. He's a proud father of three grown children: Daniel, Richard, and Alyssa.

ENDNOTES

1   John Maxwell, *Becoming a Person of Influence* (USA: Thomas Nelson, 1997), 26.

2   Roger Connors, Craig Hickman, and Tom Smith, *The Oz Principle* (New York: Portfolio/Penguin, 2004), 48.

3   Mark Samuel, *Making Yourself Indispensable* (New York: Portfolio/Penguin, 2012), 36-37.

4   Mark Sanborn, *The Fred Factor* (USA: Doubleday, 2004), 9.

5   Mark Samuel, *Making Yourself Indispensable* (New York: Portfolio/Penguin, 2012), 132.

6   Daniel Goleman, *Emotional Intelligence* (London: Bloomsbury, 1996), 56.

7   Price Pritchett, *Hard Optimism* (New York: McGraw Hill, 2007), 1.

8   Daniel Goleman, *Emotional Intelligence* (London: Bloomsbury, 1996), 36.

9   Eric Jordan, *Emotional Intelligence Mastery* (United Kingdom: Pine Peak Publishing, 2016), 8.

10 Tasha Eurich, *Insight* (London: Pan Books, 2018), 8.

11 Tasha Eurich, *Insight* (London: Pan Books, 2018), 52-53.

12 Ian Tuhovsky, *Emotional Intelligence* (USA: CreateSpace, 2017), 46-47.

13 Susan David, *Emotional Agility* (United Kingdom: Penguin Life, 2016), 18.

14 Susan David, *Emotional Agility* (United Kingdom: Penguin Life, 2016), 113-114.

15 Ryan Holiday, *Ego is the Enemy* (New York: Penguin, 2016), 118.

16 Jim Harter and Rodd Wagner, *12: The Elements of Great Managing* (USA: Gallup Press, 2006), 112.

17 Bill George, *Discover Your True North* (New Jersey: John Wiley & Sons, 2015), 123.

18 Tasha Eurich, *Insight* (London: Pan Books, 2018), 162.

19 Ryan Holiday, *Ego is the Enemy* (New York: Penguin, 2016), 4.

20 Justin Bariso, *EQ Applied* (Germany: Borough Hall, 2018), 64.

21 Justin Bariso, *EQ Applied* (Germany: Borough Hall, 2018), 55.

22 Eric Jordan, *Emotional Intelligence Mastery* (United Kingdom: Pine Peak Publishing, 2016), 36-37.

23 Susan David, *Emotional Agility* (United Kingdom: Penguin Life, 2016), 94.

24 Bill George, *Discover Your True North* (New Jersey: John Wiley & Sons, 2015), 46.

25 Ryan Holiday, *Ego is the Enemy* (New York: Penguin, 2016), 4-5.

26 Ian Tuhovsky, *Emotional Intelligence* (USA: CreateSpace, 2017), 124.

27 Martin Seligman, *Learned Optimism* (London: Nicholas Brealey Publishing, 2018), 6-7.

28 Martin Seligman, *Learned Optimism* (London: Nicholas Brealey Publishing, 2018), 220.

29 Steve Peters, *The Chimp Paradox* (United Kingdom: Vermillion, 2020), 15-16.

30 Dennis Greenberger and Christine Padesky, *Mind Over Mood* (New York: The Guilford Press, 2016), 139.

31 Dennis Greenberger and Christine Padesky, *Mind Over Mood* (New York: The Guilford Press, 2016), 17.

32 Daniel Goleman, *Emotional Intelligence* (London: Bloomsbury, 1996), 60.

33 Carol Dweck, *Mindset* (New York: Random House, 2006), 32.

34 Martin Seligman, *Learned Optimism* (London: Nicholas Brealey Publishing, 2018), 48.

35 Susan David, *Emotional Agility* (United Kingdom: Penguin Life, 2016), 38.

36 Carol Dweck, *Mindset* (New York: Random House, 2006), 11.

37 Susan David, *Emotional Agility* (United Kingdom: Penguin Life, 2016), 71.

38 Price Pritchett, *Hard Optimism* (New York: McGraw Hill, 2007), 63.

39 Price Pritchett, *Hard Optimism* (New York: McGraw Hill, 2007), 98.

40 Martin Seligman, *Learned Optimism* (London: Nicholas Brealey Publishing, 2018), 5.

41 Thibault Meurisse, *Master Your Emotions* (USA: Independently Published, 2018), 7-8.

42 Daniel Goleman, *Emotional Intelligence* (London: Bloomsbury, 1996), 87.

43 Martin Seligman, *Learned Optimism* (London: Nicholas Brealey Publishing, 2018), 217-218.

44 Jeff Keller, *Attitude Is Everything* (USA: INTI Publishing, 1999), 71.

45 Ryan Holiday, *Ego is the Enemy* (New York: Penguin, 2016), 117.

46 Justin Bariso, *EQ Applied* (Germany: Borough Hall, 2018), 114-115.

47 Thibault Meurisse, *Master Your Emotions* (USA: Independently Published, 2018), 134-135.

48 Elizabeth Day, *Failosophy* (London: 4th Estate, 2020), 6.

49 Mark McGuinness, *Resilience* (USA: Lateral Action Books, 2013), 27.

50 Jeff Keller, *Attitude is Everything* (USA: INTI Publishing, 1999), 51.

51 W. Clement Stone, *Success Through a Positive Mental Attitude* (London: Thorsons, 1990), 32.

52 Elizabeth Day, *Failosophy* (London: 4th Estate, 2020), 4.

53 John Miller, *QBQ! The Question Behind The Question* (USA: Denver Press, 2001), 26-27.

54 Ryan Holiday, *The Obstacle is the Way* (New York: Portfolio, 2014), 11.

55 Steve Pavlina, *Personal Development for Smart People* (New York: Hay House Inc, 2008), 52.

56 Mark McGuinness, *Resilience* (USA: Lateral Action Books, 2013), 93.

57 Mark Samuel, *Making Yourself Indispensable* (New York: Portfolio/Penguin, 2012), 130-131.

58 Susan David, *Emotional Agility* (United Kingdom: Penguin Life, 2016), 67.

59 William Bridges, *The Way of Transition* (USA: Da Capo Press, 2001), 1.

60 William Bridges, *The Way of Transition* (USA: Da Capo Press, 2001), 35-36.

61 Ryan Holiday, *The Obstacle is the Way* (New York: Portfolio, 2014), 44.

62 Justin Bariso, *EQ Applied* (Germany: Borough Hall, 2018), 10-11.

63 Mark Sanborn, *The Fred Factor* (USA: Doubleday, 2004), 46.

64 Daniel Goleman, *Emotional Intelligence* (London: Bloomsbury, 1996), 120.

65 Mark Sanborn, *The Fred Factor* (USA: Doubleday, 2004), 47.

66 W. Clement Stone, *Success Through a Positive Mental Attitude* (London: Thorsons, 1990), 126.

67 John Maxwell, *How to Influence People* (USA: Thomas Nelson, 2013), 65.

68 John Maxwell, *Becoming a Person of Influence* (USA: Thomas Nelson, 1997), 64.

69 John Maxwell, *Becoming a Person of Influence* (USA: Thomas Nelson, 1997), 38-39.

70 Joseph Grenny, Ron McMillian, Kerry Patterson, and Al Switzler *Crucial Conversations* (New York: McGraw, Hill, 2002), 13.

71 Justin Bariso, *EQ Applied* (Germany: Borough Hall, 2018), 102.

72 Joseph Grenny, Ron McMillian, Kerry Patterson, and Al Switzler *Crucial Conversations* (New York: McGraw, Hill, 2002), 65-93.

73 Joseph Grenny, Ron McMillian, Kerry Patterson, and Al Switzler *Crucial Conversations* (New York: McGraw, Hill, 2002), 20.

74 Ryan Holiday, *Ego is the Enemy* (New York: Penguin, 2016), 105.

75 John Maxwell, *Talent is Never Enough* (USA: Thomas Nelson, 2007), 172.

76 Steve Pavlina, *Personal Development for Smart People* (New York: Hay House Inc, 2008), 3.

77 Randy Pausch, *The Last Lecture* (USA: Disney Educational Publications).

78 Mark Samuel, *Making Yourself Indispensable* (New York: Portfolio/Penguin, 2012), 155.

79 Peter Hollins, *The Science of Rapid Skill Acquisition* (Great Britain: Independently Publishing, 2019), 110-116.

80 Brian Tracy, *The Power of Self-Confidence* (USA: Wiley, 2012), 97.

81 Brian Tracy, *The Power of Self-Confidence* (USA: Wiley, 2012), 95.

82 Mark Kizilos, *Framebreaking Leadership Development* (USA: Experience-Based Development Associates LLC, 2012).

83 Brian Tracy, *The Power of Self-Confidence* (USA: Wiley, 2012), 93.

84 John Maxwell, *The 15 Invaluable Laws of Growth* (New York: Center Street, 2012), 91.

85 John Maxwell, *The 15 Invaluable Laws of Growth* (New York: Center Street, 2012), 93.

86 Ryan Holiday, *Ego is the Enemy* (New York: Penguin, 2016), 38-39.

87 John Maxwell, *The 15 Invaluable Laws of Growth* (New York: Center Street, 2012), 54.

88 Thibault Meurisse, *Success* (USA: Independently Published, 2007), 1.

89 Linda Galindo, *The 85% Solution* (San Francisco: Jossey-Bass, 2009), 92.

90 Bill George, *Discover Your True North* (New Jersey: John Wiley & Sons, 2015), 123.

91 Lee J. Colan, *Engaging the Hearts and Minds of All Your Employees* (New York: McGraw-Hill, 2017), 15.

92 Chip Heath and Dan Heath, *Switch* (New York: Random House, 2010), 222.

93 Ryan Holiday, *Ego is the Enemy* (New York: Penguin, 2016), 79.

94 Diana Whitney, *Appreciative Leadership* (New York: McGraw Hill, 2010), 128-129.

A free ebook edition is available with the purchase of this book.

To claim your free ebook edition:

Visit MorganJamesBOGO.com
Sign your name CLEARLY in the space
Complete the form and submit a photo of
the entire copyright page
You or your friend can download the ebook
to your preferred device

Morgan James
BOGO™

A **FREE** ebook edition is available for you
or a friend with the purchase of this print book.

CLEARLY SIGN YOUR NAME ABOVE

Instructions to claim your free ebook edition:
1. Visit MorganJamesBOGO.com
2. Sign your name CLEARLY in the space above
3. Complete the form and submit a photo
   of this entire page
4. You or your friend can download the ebook
   to your preferred device

Print & Digital Together Forever.

Snap a photo

Free ebook

Read anywhere

CPSIA information can be obtained
at www.ICGtesting.com
Printed in the USA
JSHW040744120322
23840JS00001B/13